SCENES

from the

COMMON WEALTH

Short Plays & Monologues
by Kentucky Women

EDITED BY
Shan R. Ayers, MFA

**MOTES
BOOKS**

Scenes from the Common Wealth:
Short Plays & Monologues by Kentucky Women

Shan R. Ayers, ed.

ANTHOLOGY
ISBN   978-1-934894-48-4

Profits from the sale of this book contribute to the MotesBooks-Kentucky Voices Fund, which provides small grants for the development of independent theatre in Kentucky.

Anne Shelby attributes Gershwin, Berlin and Greaney for select phrases from songs they wrote.

CAUTION: *This book contains literary versions of the scripts it comprises. These are not acting scripts. Purchase of this book in no way grants the purchaser or reader the right to perform these plays or read portions of the texts aloud in public. This book may not be used for theatrical productions or for staged readings. For permission to produce one of the plays in this anthology, please contact the playwright or her agent directly.*

Book Design
EYE.K

Published in Kentucky by
MOTES BOOKS

www.MOTESBOOKS.com

PRINTED & BOUND IN THE USA

ACKNOWLEDGEMENTS

I would be remiss if I did not include some sort of acknowledgements and words of gratitude. First of all, I would like to thank the writers whose work is included in this collection. Their unselfish sharing has given new material to the theatre world. My thanks to Dr. Verlaine McDonald, my department chair, for her support; she assisted me in securing a sabbatical leave to complete this collection. I acknowledge my daughters, Angela Joseph and Ashley Ayers—both of whom inherited a love of theatre and grew up surrounded by my work—for their continued love and support. Most importantly, my wife, Trish Ayers, allowed me to hear the words of the playwrights she was mentoring and understood why I spent so much time on this project. Finally, I would like to dedicate this collection to the memory of my mother, Rosemary Ayers, who instilled in me a respect for the contributions of the women of the world.

– SRA

CONTENTS

The Context

The Scenes

FOREWORD

"Unique Takes on Universal Stories"

It has been said that a play about a woman and daughter is a woman's play, while one about a father and son is a universal story. As if plays by women do not address basic human themes. As if had it been *Death of a Saleswoman* perhaps no male need bother with it. But the works in this collection put lie to that sentiment. This collection of powerful plays by Kentucky women resonates with each playwright's unique take on universal stories.

The themes in this collection of scripts include the devastating impact of self delusion, the link between mortality and dignity, between morality and death, the bonds of family, and how hiding secrets destroys lives. These plays examine the healing paths taken or not taken, paths acknowledged or paths overlooked, and they embrace what is most important in life.

As with Willie Loman, eight of these plays address the dire implications of self delusion. In Arlene Hutton's *Remedial Lessons*, a professor fails to see what's right in front of her. The beauty queen in Brenda White's *Southern Beauty* fails to anticipate what will happen when her looks fade. A mother's chilling blindness to the danger a predatory preacher poses to her daughters resonates in *The Baptizing* by Denise R. McKinney. A desperate woman in Beth Dotson-Brown's *Stranger on the Porch* convinces herself that a deception is truth. In Gail Livesay's *Ward 101*, the only healing path a patient finds is the sanctuary of an imaginary friend. The misguided hope that her boyfriend will return for her leaves a young woman stunningly vulnerable in Nancy Gall-Clayton's *The Fish in the Dumpster*. In Sallie Bingham's *No Time*, three friends' interpretations of their world are so limited that they skews the audience's perception of what is happening. And in the monologue from *The Honey Harvest* by Liz Fentress, a woman's denial of her plight results in painful stings.

Myriad poignant and challenging issues surrounding death are explored in five of these plays. Linda Caldwell portrays how critical it is to allow loved ones to die with dignity in *Homespun*. Sacrifices made to provide for ill and dying family members pile up in Trish Ayers' *Painting the Egress*. *Sacred Secrets*, by bell hooks, probes how remembering and learning from our ancestors enriches our lives. The morality of collateral damage during warfare is movingly and metaphorically depicted in Naomi Wallace's *One Short Sleepe*. The life-affirming support a community provides to a woman facing devastating illness underlies Constance Alexander's *The Way Home*.

The life-damaging impact of hiding secrets in Carolyn Bertram-Arnold's *A Home Like No Place* rings a warning toll. And finally, the themes of staying positive because you don't know what's down the river and valuing what's best about life shimmer in Anne Shelby's *Remembering Rosemary* and Belinda Mason's *The Gifts of the Spirit*.

Thank you to MotesBooks and to the MotesBooks-Kentucky Voices Fund for supporting Kentucky women playwrights. The plays in this collection are to be savored and reread and pondered over time. The voices herein are varied and lyrical and strong, and the stories are compelling and intricate and universal.

HEIDI SAUNDERS' award-winning plays include:
Sex Again (2012 Roots of the Bluegrass New Plays finalist),
War Games (2012 Kentucky Playwrights Workshop New Play Contest finalist),
and *Pump Works* (2010 Roots of the Bluegrass New Play finalist).
She is a member of Dramatists Guild, Times Square Playwrights
and Kentucky Playwrights Workshop.
She divides her time between Fisherville, Kentucky, and New York.

Introduction

"These Are Not 'Women's Plays'"

Why collect plays by women? Well, for the most part, history reveals to us that theatre has been particularly unfair to women by too often excluding them from participating in the collaborative art of theatre.

Because women were not "citizens" of ancient Greece or Rome, some sources indicate that they were forbidden even from attending the theatre. Not until well after the Renaissance were women allowed to participate legally in theatrical performance, and then only in limited ways. Most sources have the earliest recorded woman playwright as being Hrosvitha of Gandersheim, a 10th century nun who wrote dramatic adaptations of liturgical stories that were never produced during her lifetime.

Other records of women's contributions to the canon of dramatic literature are sketchy, at best. Research shows that women writers began getting noticed in the late 17th and early 18th centuries, but not nearly to the same acclaim as male writers. Perhaps the most well-known of these playwriting women was Aphra Behn, who has been called England's first professional woman writer.

Inequities against women were carried into the next few centuries in many aspects of theatre. In the United States, it wasn't until 1998 that a woman won the coveted Tony Award for Best Director and Best Director for a Musical. In the February 2008 issue of *American Theatre*, Eric Bentley is quoted as saying, "There are plenty of good writers around, and the arrival of women writers as a new force is interesting, culturally, and positive." The phrase "new force" is the key to his statement that women writers have become a positive element in contemporary theatre.

What is particularly interesting about Bentley's statement is that women writers have been creating new work quite rapidly, but these new works are not seeing productions as readily as work by male writers. In her introduction to *Women Writing Plays*, Marsha Norman makes this observation: "In my lifetime, in America, women writing plays has gone from nearly unheard of to nearly commonplace. Unfortunately, the producing of plays by women has not made the same leap." Norman goes on to quote a 2002 New York State Council on the Arts paper—*Report on the Status of Women in Theatre: A Limited Engagement?*—saying that the report found "consistently low main stage participation of women playwrights and directors, particularly among theatres with higher budgets."

What is particularly troubling is that the report also reflects a similar low statistic when looking at seasons of theatres dedicated to producing new plays. In many cases, these theatres report having produced no new plays by women.

Report on the Status of Women: A Limited Engagement? authors Susan Jonas and Suzanne Bennett report that *Time Out* reviewer Sam Whitehead was surprised when he saw Margaret Edison's play, *Wit*. He said, "While it was about a woman, and a woman's problems, it was really about a human predicament." He goes on to state that he had expected to see a "whining victim play." In the *Village Voice*, Alisa Solomon responded by asking if anyone "considered *Oedipus Rex* 'a whiny victim play.'" Isn't it time for us to remove the gender descriptor when classifying plays according to their creator?

Upon receiving the second Susan Smith Blackburn Prize (an award presented to women playwrights yearly since 1979), Barbara Schneider commented, "... I also believe that twenty years from now, the words 'woman playwright' will seem to us entirely outmoded and completely unfashionable." I would like to agree with Schneider, but we are thirty years past her comment and we still have these gender divisions in playwriting.

As recently as 2010, when the annual Tony award nominations were announced, Teresa Rebeck, playwright and member of Dramatists Guild, asked, "Where are the women?" In response to her great question, albeit sad that it was necessary to ask, the Dramatists Guild rallied and developed the first ever Lillian Hellman Awards for Outstanding Achievement by Women in the Theatre. In a hastily organized ceremony, done on a borrowed stage in between crew calls, Christopher Durang hosted these perhaps annual but hopefully soon to be unnecessary awards. Presenters and winners ranged from playwrights whose work is currently playing in the commercial theatre, to writers who have won the Pulitzer, to designers and directors who have made an impact on the work of women writers. A plethora of attendees were present to celebrate the work of women.

It seems that the term "woman playwright" is still, seemingly and unfortunately, fashionable.

Many short plays, especially ten-minute plays, are not produced as frequently or with the same production attention paid to them as other plays. Certainly, commercial venues would have a hard time making their budget on season after season of short or ten-minute plays. However, many companies are having short play contests, the most famous held in Kentucky at Actors Theatre of Louisville. Writers get advice from directors, actors, critics and audience. But it can be maddening for writers to sift through all of this criticism. More than one writer has indicated that hearing her work in a reading does not necessarily lead to rewriting marathons. A reading can indicate that the play is now ready to be fully produced and, hopefully, published so that others can benefit from the writer's creations.

One way to get these new materials read more widely is to collect them into anthologies. Certain collections cover plays that span the canon of western theatre history. Others pay service to certain types of plays: musicals, plays about America, gay/lesbian plays and, like this anthology, plays by women.

So, why collect plays by Kentucky women? When the writers whose work is contained in this anthology were queried about this, their responses were as varied as their plays. Some responded that Kentucky was their source of inspiration or that their muse was here. Many replied by saying that they found a supportive community of like-minded artist and writers. One admitted that she has never lived anywhere else and that her husband has never lived farther than one-half mile from where he was raised. One took a school trip to New York and enjoyed herself but could not wait to return to the tranquility of her rural home. A few traced their roots to Kentucky and feel anchored here, whether or not they reside in the Commonwealth. Interestingly, one of the writers spoke fondly of her Kentucky heritage but noted that she knew at an early age that to be successful as an independent woman and a successful writer, she would need to leave in order to fulfill her dreams. Some find comfort in being here. Others, while acknowledging their indebtedness to their Kentucky connections, enjoy and seek the opportunities beyond its borders. All of the writers included in *Scenes from the Common Wealth: Short Plays & Monologues by Kentucky Women* felt it necessary to fuse their other writings into their playwriting, to fuse their cultural heritage or residence in Kentucky into their writing in some fashion. Many of the writers are also poets, and they draw on that poetic muse to create their lyrical, heartfelt and dead-on dialogue.

This anthology was initially inspired when I read plays created during a Kentucky Women Playwrights Seminar funded, in part, by the Kentucky Foundation for Women. Headed by Berea playwright Trish Ayers, this seminar led a group of women through the initial processes of playwriting (and has regularly inspired subsequent sessions) but ended up giving them much more than a new writing skill. As I heard about those particular plays (a few are included in this book), listened to them being read in monthly public readings and talked to those writers about their work, it occurred to me that many were getting to the heart of a personal issue, revealing something they needed to get out, sharing something from which they needed to be unburdened. In a sense, some writers who created their plays from an autobiographical event did so for more than performance; it was salve, an emotional release, a closing of a deep wound.

Those writers whose work is entirely fictional deal with deep issues, as well. There are many specific topics, yes, but they all hold universal meanings. None of these are "whiny victims' plays." The writers are telling things that need told, many in a serious voice, others incorporating humor.

As one of only a few males who regularly attended those monthly readings, I often served as a reader, and I had the opportunity to breathe life into some of these beautiful characters for the first time. If my voice gave life to a character that helped to heal a broken spirit, then I feel humbled. But I was not there as a man educated in theatre or giving direction to those writers. I was there because new writers need support. New scripts need opportunity. New voices need a sounding board. My gender and education were of no importance. My presence was.

Other writers, whose work is included here but who were not involved in the Kentucky Women Playwrights Seminar, offer the same sort of inspiration.

It is important to point out that these are not "women's plays." Rather, they are plays that have been written by women. Yes, this anthology is limited to plays written by women specifically tied to Kentucky, but the packaging is simply to allow for greater focus on these works by these women. We have too many anthologies dedicated to the usual canon of "dead white male" playwrights, and their plays are never labeled "men's plays."

SHAN R. AYERS, editor of *Scenes from the Common Wealth: Short Plays & Monologues by Kentucky Women,* has been a professor of theatre at Berea College in Kentucky since 1984. His playwriting career began in the mid-1990s when he and his spouse, Trish Ayers, co-authored *Circle of Voices,* a play that dramatizes seven Native American stories. He also wrote *Draped in Honor,* produced in 2007 by the Berea Arts Council, *How Many Times,* performed in the Kentucky Playwrights Workshop 2012 new play contest, and *With No Where to Go.* Shan has taught playwriting at Berea and in Japan and Italy. He has an M.F.A. in theatre and is an associate member of the Dramatists Guild.

Remedial Lessons

ARLENE HUTTON

Characters:
SUSAN   40s or 50s, an academic
LAURA   25-40, graduate student, severe cerebral palsy, in a wheelchair

Time: Present
Place: A university
Setting: Corridor in a classroom building

[At rise, there is a bench or a couple of chairs against the wall outside a classroom door. SUSAN, a teacher, enters pushing LAURA, a graduate student, in a wheelchair. A tote bag hangs from the back of the chair. LAURA has severe cerebral palsy, and it is not always possible to understand her speech, although she tries hard. LAURA has a good sense of humor.]

SUSAN: Here we are. Here's 106. Oops, the door's closed.
LAURA: *[LAURA tries to point to her watch.]* Early.
SUSAN: Is this the right room? Class started already?
LAURA: We're early.
SUSAN: Is this right?
LAURA: Three. Three o'clock.
SUSAN: Three o'clock? But it's only two-thirty. Oh, the class starts at
               three.
LAURA: *[Nods.]*

SUSAN:	So we're early.
LAURA:	*[Nods again.]*
SUSAN:	Oh. *[SUSAN looks at her watch.]* We didn't have to rush after all.
LAURA:	No.
SUSAN:	That's what you were trying to tell me, wasn't it?
LAURA:	Yes.
SUSAN:	And I thought you said to hurry!
LAURA:	I said "early."
SUSAN:	Early. Of course. Well, we'll just have to wait, won't we?
LAURA:	You don't have to.
SUSAN:	I don't have any appointments until three-thirty.
LAURA:	You don't have to wait.
SUSAN:	Well, I can't just leave you here alone. What would you be doing if your, uh, your chair battery was working? Your, uh, chair battery. You go all over on your own—I've seen you—but what do you do if there is time between classes?
LAURA:	Wait.
SUSAN:	I could take you to the library, but by the time we got back there it would almost be time to bring you back here again. Would you like to go to the library?
LAURA:	No.
SUSAN:	No. That wouldn't make sense.
LAURA:	I'm okay alone.
SUSAN:	That's okay. I'll wait. I was happy to help you. Got me out of the building. I don't get out of my building often enough. Nice to get to another part of the campus. I can't believe the students all just walked out of class and left you sitting there.
LAURA:	They're young.
SUSAN:	They're immature. *[Pause.]* Would you like something to drink while we wait? There's a machine. We passed a machine. It's on me. What would you like? *[SUSAN pulls change from pocket.]*
LAURA:	No.
SUSAN:	Coke? Be right back. *[Exits. LAURA is alone on stage.*
SUSAN:	*[Enters with a Pepsi and a diet Seven-up or Sprite.]* No Coke. But they had Pepsi. *[Starts to hand it to LAURA.]*
LAURA:	Thank you. *[Clumsily takes the Pepsi and holds it in her lap.]*
SUSAN:	Shall I open it for you?
LAURA:	No, thanks.
SUSAN:	Don't you want it? I'll open it for you.
LAURA:	No. No straw.
SUSAN:	Oh, you need a straw.
LAURA:	But I'm not thirsty right now.
SUSAN:	You said you didn't want anything, didn't you?

LAURA:	Yes.
SUSAN:	I'm sorry. I misunderstood you. I'm sorry. Of course you couldn't. You can drink it later. Here, I'll put it in your bag for later. *[Takes the can and places it in a bag on the back of LAURA's chair. Sits on the bench, her own unopened can next to her.]*
LAURA:	Drink your soda.
SUSAN:	What?
LAURA:	*[Pointing.]* Drink your soda.
SUSAN:	You want it?
LAURA:	You, you, you drink it.
SUSAN:	Oh, all right. *[Opens it and drinks a few sips. There is an awkward silence for a moment.]* You made an A on that test. And your papers are excellent.
LAURA:	Thank you.
SUSAN:	You're the best student I have. In all my classes, you're the best student. Is someone helping you write your papers? It's okay if you have help, you know.
LAURA:	No help.
SUSAN:	What I don't understand is why you are in a remedial class. You're better than some of my graduate students.
LAURA:	I AM a graduate student.
SUSAN:	You shouldn't be in a remedial class. I didn't know, because you don't speak up in class, what a, what a scholar you are. I don't give papers or tests until mid-terms—maybe I should, but it's so much to grade—and I didn't know you could, you could write like that, or understand the test questions so well. You shouldn't be in, well, why are you in a remedial English class?
LAURA:	Dr. Hillard.
SUSAN:	What? I'm so sorry. I didn't get that.
LAURA:	Dr. Hillard.
SUSAN:	Dr. Hillard? Dr. William P. Hillard? Old Will P.? Dear old Dr. Will P. put you in my remedial class?
LAURA:	Instead of my thesis lab.
SUSAN:	You can't take a required lab because you had to take my class?
LAURA:	*[Nods.]*
SUSAN :	You would have finished this year? Your what? B.A.? No, M.A.?
LAURA:	*[Nods again.]*
SUSAN:	You're getting your masters and you have to go for an extra semester because you are in my remedial English class? What a joke.
LAURA:	Not funny.
SUSAN:	No, no, no. It is funny. It's unbelievably funny. You should know this. You've got to hear this. Dr. Hillard, William P. Hillard, as he calls himself, Will P., as we call him, is trying to

get rid of me. He can hire two adjuncts for my salary with no benefits. Two for the price of one. And no tenure problems, either, no sir. But I won't take early retirement—I won't get anything later on—so Dr. Will P changes my schedule, tries to give me remedial classes. But they won't make. My classes won't make. The students don't sign up—rather take, well, they hear how easy Lawton's classes are, or Brown's, so they sign up for them. My remedial classes don't make. My 401s and 500s and 602s, no problem, they're full all the time—can't get adjuncts to teach that. My graduate classes make, fill up, if he offers them. But he doesn't. He gives me remedial classes and they don't make. So last year I had only two classes, one a practicum and, well, I had the time, so I wrote a book. Will P is livid. I'm publishing—looks good to the faculty review—and he's trying to get me out.

LAURA: You're a good teacher.

SUSAN: You should know this. The next semester, same thing, my remedial classes don't make—only one graduate class, and it's got a waiting list. I have the time, I speak at conferences. Every weekend I'm traveling. Will P can't stand it. *[She looks at LAURA.]* Do you want to hear all this? So this semester my remedial classes don't make again, but one class, the two o'clock, that one is one student shy of qualifying. No other remedial classes are offered at that time. They are all eight a.m. or evening classes. It's the only afternoon class. That's why it nearly makes. Has almost enough students. At the last minute one more student is added. Dr. Hillard adds one more student and the class makes.

LAURA: Me.

SUSAN: You shouldn't have been in the class. If I had known—you could have left during Drop and Add, but you never said anything.

LAURA: *[Shrugs.]*

SUSAN: My class, my very first freshman remedial class makes because Dr. Hillard puts a graduate student in it. What a laugh. And so I've been playing catch-up all semester because I've never taught a remedial class before. It's been lots of work.

LAURA: You're a good teacher.

SUSAN: I didn't get that.

LAURA: Good teacher. You're a good teacher.

SUSAN: I am a good teacher. I'm a very good teacher.

LAURA: Why don't you quit?

SUSAN: Why don't I quit?

LAURA: Yes.

SUSAN: Tenure. Security. I don't know. I've never taught anywhere else. Went here for undergrad, got a fellowship for my M.A. and Ph.D., got hired. Dr. Hillard was my mentor, isn't that a laugh. That old alcoholic has-been. *[Pause.]* He's only chair on a technicality. The dean wanted me, the president wanted me, the faculty wanted me, but he pulled a deal somehow. Had to give it to him. They told me behind closed doors. In public—how he had been a leader in this department. Whoop-de-do. Led a lot of women around, that's what he did. You didn't hear me say that.

LAURA: He's bad.

SUSAN: Promises anything. I can't believe he put you in my remedial class. I am so sorry. *[Pause.]* What now, after you finish here?

LAURA: Harvard.

SUSAN: Harvard? You're going on to Harvard?

LAURA: *[Nods.]*

SUSAN: Another masters degree?

LAURA: Ph.D.

SUSAN: Ph.D.?

LAURA: Yes.

SUSAN: Well! I hope you get in.

LAURA: Fellowship.

SUSAN: You'll need a fellowship.

LAURA: *[Shakes her head.]*

SUSAN: You've GOT a fellowship.

LAURA: Yes.

SUSAN: You have a fellowship for a doctorate at Harvard and you're in my freshman remedial class?

LAURA: Yes. *[Pause.]*

SUSAN: I wanted to go to Harvard. Hillard wouldn't write the recommendation. So you're going to Harvard. Next fall?

LAURA: January.

SUSAN: After your thesis lab. After the extra semester here.

LAURA: Yes.

SUSAN: I am so sorry. I could have moved you out of my class. Did you talk to your advisor?

LAURA: Sabbatical.

SUSAN: On sabbatical. What about the registrar?

LAURA: *[Throws up her hands.]*

SUSAN: I should have known. I am so sorry. I didn't know.

LAURA: *[Shrugs her shoulders.]*

SUSAN: I'm really a better teacher than that.

LAURA: You're good.

SUSAN: Not with the remedial class. That takes a certain...I don't know.

LAURA: Other class.

SUSAN: You haven't been in my class before. I'd remember.

LAURA: TV. Computer.

SUSAN: You took the TV course?

LAURA: Good.

SUSAN: That's where I remember your name. You took the remote class.

LAURA: Good lectures.

SUSAN: That was a good class. On TV. Hillard won't let me do it again. Too popular. Two hundred students signed up—we could only grade papers for one hundred and even that took away from the on-campus classes.

LAURA: I like TV classes.

SUSAN: Of course. I didn't think about how students like you...well, disabled students— They discontinued the program. Hillard's classes barely made. He didn't get his extra class for bonus pay. I never get a bonus class. Never make overtime. Never get a summer class—that's where you really make your money—Hillard always takes it for himself. Takes everything. My classes. My top students. Takes credit for my projects. My graduate research for his own journal submissions. Took my office and made me share with the adjuncts. Took my ideas, my youth, my virginity. My, my, my—

LAURA: *[Slowly and distinctly.]* Why are you here?

SUSAN: What did you say?

LAURA: Why are you still here?

SUSAN: Why am I still here? I'm waiting to take you into your class.

                        [Blackout.]
                        [End.]

AUTHOR NOTE *from playwright* ARLENE HUTTON

My first job out of grad school was in the English department of
a community college, where I befriended Laura, a young woman with
cerebral palsy. Her battery-powered chair frequently broke down,
and on those days I would wheel her to her next class. Laura's sense of
humor was infectious; we had some very good times, telling each other
such silly stories that sometimes we would be laughing too hard to enter
the building for her next class. She was by far the most brilliant student
I knew but, as she told me, was often dismissed by people who didn't
take time to try and understand her halting speech. One professor would
ignore Laura, giving instructions to his secretary to repeat to Laura,
even though she was in the same room and could hear him perfectly well.

Years later I thought of her and wrote *Remedial Lessons*,
loosely basing one of the characters on Laura and creating another who is
mostly fiction. In spite of her good intentions, Susan, the professor,
while appearing capable on the outside, is a mess of a woman inside,
nervous and bitter, never looking past her own problems.
Laura, who has far more physical challenges in life,
is moving forward with her dreams and achieving her goals.

Many of my plays are about an exchange of power between women.
In *Remedial Lessons* I explore that dynamic, showing that
things are rarely what they seem. I want to present a disability on stage
and let us see how even a well-meaning person can be
thoughtless and dismissive. Laura has little to learn from Susan;
Susan has everything to learn from Laura, if she will only stop and listen.
The student becomes the teacher,
and the teacher, hopefully, learns an important lesson.

Southern Beauty

Brenda K. White

Character:
SANDY   25, a voluptuous, former beauty pageant regular.

Time: Present
Place: A nice suburban home
Setting: SANDY's trophy room

[At rise, SANDY, a voluptuous 25-year-old, is surveying herself in a full-length mirror, pondering her life among remnants of her beauty pageant career: gowns, trophies, tiaras, swimsuits, full-length mirrors, batons, sheet music, etc.]

SANDY: I'm beautiful. *[Turns to audience.]* That's what everybody tells me. I know it, too. When I look in the mirror *[Glances at mirror.]* I see what men like and women envy. Elizabeth Taylor eyes, Bo Derek cheeks, Angelina Jolie lips, Marilyn Monroe tits and ass, Scarlett O'Hara waist. I'm the purr in purple, the go in indigo. I'm sugar, spice and everything nice. I'm beautiful and I know it. *[Turns to audience.]*
Mama said to me, 'Girl'—I was six at the time—'you got beauty and you better learn how to use it.' I think she knew the women in our family would never, in no way, shape, form or fashion, be MENSA material. *[Beat.]* 'You got it,' Mama said, 'you gotta flaunt it.' Daddy had been long

gone by that time. *[Beat.]* I never actually knew Daddy. *[Beat.]* Maybe there never was no Daddy. *[Puzzles a moment as if it's the first time she's contemplated it, then shakes it off.]*

Anyhow, from the get-go it's just been Mama and me and all them beauty pageants. I took first place in little ol' Clarkston County Fair when I was six. That got Mama really pumped. I'd be nowhere if it weren't for Mama. *[Beat.]* From then on it was gymnastics, tap dancing, baton twirling and voice lessons. At home, I walked with a book on my head so I could learn to walk down a runway like my head and neck are not attached to the rest of my body, my legs gliding forward through some mysterious force of their own, practicing a Queen Elizabeth wave to adoring fans and commoners alike. You know them. *[Condescends to audience.]*

Now there's only so far you can go with the beauty queen thing. It's not like there's job openings for former beauty queens, with 401Ks and full-coverage health insurance. Some beauty queens, like me, didn't go to college. Some moved to big cities, became exotic dancers, got hooked on cocaine. Said it gave them energy to dance. Some ended up in porn movies after being chewed up and spit out by Hollywood.

Me, I stayed on in Clarkston County, opened a beauty school training program. I teach the fine art of fashion and proper etiquette for all occasions along with gymnastics, tap dancing, baton twirling, piano and voice lessons. I call it Sandy's Southern Beauty School.

Two years ago, I married Dr. Jack Swinson. He's an Ob/Gyn. Every little girl he delivers, why, that's a potential southern beauty, or at least a southern beauty wannabe. I'm the second, younger version Mrs. Swinson. *[Beat.]* Some are a-saying I'm a trophy wife, but it's not true. I can't help it if the first Mrs. Swinson got frumpy and feminist all at the same time. *[Beat.]* Well, she doesn't live in Clarkston County anymore. Moved off to some artist colony in Santa Fe. *[Waves hand dismissively.]* Jack called it a menopausal uprising. *[Beat.]* I call it crazy.

Jack calls me his little southern beauty. That's how I came up with the name for my beauty school—Sandy's Southern Beauty School. Next year I'm expanding—Sandy's Southern Beauty School of Tackett County. That was Jack's idea. I'd be nowhere if it weren't for Jack. He said to me, 'Girl,'—I was twenty-two at the time—'you got beauty and you better learn how to use it.' Sandy's Southern Beauty School was born right then and there. When I walk into a room on Jack's arm, he introduces me as his southern beauty. Heads turn. Jack likes that. In return, I get my beauty schools and free pap smears for the rest of my life.

[End.]

AUTHOR NOTE *from playwright* BRENDA K. WHITE

◇◇

Sandy, a prodigy of beauty pageant boot camp, is not a
character that I easily identify with on a personal level.
In the process of writing *Southern Beauty*, much to my surprise,
I gained empathy and tolerance for her which led to
admiration for her shrewdness as well as her
survivalism on a more universal level.
Pragmatic and resilient, Sandy will succeed on her own terms.

The Baptizing

Denise R. McKinney

Characters:

DAMARIS	16, an Appalachian Kentucky girl who trusts her intuition even if she can't always describe the depth of her spiritual questioning and journey. An obedient daughter, but she voices her thoughts and opinions.
MADELINE	35-40, DAMARIS' mother who feels societal and Biblical pressure to "raise her girls right," although she is not without empathy for DAMARIS.
TAMARA	14, DAMARIS' sister who provides a lighter way of looking at both DAMARIS' and MADELINE's viewpoints.
BROTHER BOYD	70-75, a circuit preacher and pedophile. His actions are covert, so adult members of the congregation put up with him. DAMARIS hates him.

Time:	Present
Place:	Appalachian Kentucky
Setting:	Small church and creek

MADELINE:	*[Turning to DAMARIS.]* The Bible says to repent and be baptized, Damaris! *[Starts to unbutton DAMARIS' dress from the back.]*
DAMARIS:	Don't say when, Ma. Why can't it wait?
TAMARA:	Oh, Lordy. Here we go! *[Pulls the curtains over all the outer*

windows.] Don't want to give them Scott boys something to look at!

MADELINE: Tam, don't you start. *[Beat.]* Damaris, it was bad enough that you said, "Guess so," when preacher asked if you repented of your sins. Why can't you just do this for me?

DAMARIS: *[Slipping out of her dress with just her slip on.]* Didn't know a baptizing was for anybody except the one getting baptized. And maybe for the Lord.

MADELINE: I've worked so hard with you two girls. What will people think? Here you are, sixteen years old and just now getting baptized. Please don't give me no flack.

TAMARA: *[Takes a hand-held fan and sits down on a main level pew.]* Guess I got two more years, huh, Ma?

MADELINE: Hush. *[Helps DAMARIS put on the white robe.]*

DAMARIS: Ma, I don't want to be baptized. I don't want it. It makes me feel creepy.

MADELINE: You're crazy. Just go and do it.

DAMARIS: *[Turns to her mother.]* No, you're crazy. What in the world do you hope to prove by having your sixteen-year-old *[Raises her hands and uses fingers as the quotation marks sign.]* "rebel" child get baptized? Why do you care so much what people think?

MADELINE: You know how people talk, Damaris. I want them to think I've raised you right. *[Beat.]* I mean…to KNOW I've raised you right. *[Steps back to admire DAMARIS in her robe.]*

TAMARA: *[Gets up to tidy area. Folds DAMARIS' dress, puts shoes in a bag, etc.]* Ma, what does it matter? Damaris don't want to do it. That's not a reflection on you. You could even howl and moan like Aunt Pearlie does over Jimmy. *[Adopts a high pitched, mocking voice.]* "When, oh, when is-a my baby gonna get saved?!?" *[Giggles.]*

DAMARIS: Hey, yeah, ma. You say that you and Pearlie ain't got nothing in common. Me running off about now would give you all something to talk about. *[The SISTERS high-five each other and giggle.]*

MADELINE: *[Enunciating sharply.]* Why don't you just cut out my heart with a dull butcher knife? *[A beat, then a return to normal cadence.]* It'd be quicker and kinder than the fluff you and Tam are giving me now.

DAMARIS: Ma, I love you to death, but you don't understand. Brother Boyd is a pervert. Even if I did want to get baptized—and I don't—I wouldn't want him to be the one doing it.

MADELINE: *[Moves to the altar where she has a bag of supplies. Gets out a brush.]* Damaris, that old man ain't gonna hurt you. Here, sit down. Let me plait your hair.

DAMARIS: *[Sits on the altar pew as MADELINE begins to braid her hair.]* He's sick. He tried to kiss me when I wasn't even grown. You know that. I still feel like I'm gonna throw up when I shake his hand after meeting.

TAMARA: *[Sitting at the edge of the altar with feet on the floor.]* Yeah, ma. He never looks us in the eye…only looks at our boobs.

MADELINE: Tam, maybe you're the one who needs to go to the creek. I never heard such in all my life.

TAMARA: It's the truth. If you were under eighteen years old, he'd be a-pantin' after you, too. *[Leafs through altar Bible.]*

MADELINE: *[Comes from behind the pew, exasperated. DAMARIS' hair is not finished.]* All right, all right, girls. He's a creepy old codger, I'll give you that. But it don't matter who's doing the baptizing as long as you get baptized.

DAMARIS: Ma, it ain't just Preacher that makes me feel funny. *[Beat.]* I ain't ready. I ain't nearly good enough.

TAMARA: I'll say. *[Shakes the Bible at DAMARIS, teasingly.]*

MADELINE: *[More gently now, MADELINE resumes braiding DAMARIS' hair.]* Doing it will make you want to be good, Damaris. Really.

DAMARIS: Shouldn't I want to be good anyhow? I mean, shouldn't the wanting to be good come first?

MADELINE: *[A little exasperated.]* I don't know what in the world you're talking about. *[Beat.]*

TAMARA: *[Not looking up, leafing through Bible.]* That makes three of us. *[Beat.]*

DAMARIS: *[Pulls away and looks at MADELINE, although she still sits. Her hair is finished.]* I'm talking about getting baptized when I want to get baptized, not when you—or anyone else—wants me to get baptized. Feels like a lie this way.

MADELINE: *[Holds on to the back of the pew.]* The Bible don't say get baptized when you want to. The Bible just says do it. I don't see why it's so hard for you. You're really a good girl.

DAMARIS: That's what I mean, too. Ain't baptizing supposed to change you? I kinda like who I am.

TAMARA: I might go over to Mom's side. *[Gets up to open the curtains on each window.]*

DAMARIS: *[Raises her hand.]* I'm gonna slap the stupid right outta you.

MADELINE: *[Raises voice.]* Girls! *[Starts to gather bags of clothes, shoes, etc.]*

DAMARIS: *[Still sitting.]* Ma, at school I see some of those holy rollers after they get baptized. They act so stuck up. I don't want to be that way.

TAMARA: Yeah, you ought to see Marsha. She wears those floor-length skirts—with the slit all the way up to her rump—and swishes her ponytail back and forth as she walks. *[Demonstrates as she walks from window to window.]* She'll sneak out back and smoke and then preach to me how I'm going to hell for wearing jeans.

DAMARIS: *[Still sitting.]* That's part of it, too. I don't want to be fake. *[More resigned, losing some of her "fire."]* I want to get baptized when I want to get baptized, and I want to still be who I am. I don't want to change.

MADELINE: *[Prepares to exit.]* Damaris, you're getting baptized today and that's it. You can work out all the details in your head afterward. Everybody's down at the creek. You done made your confession … sort of. You can't back out now.

DAMARIS: *[Holding back, lingering in the church.]* Mom, it's not right. It's not something I want now.

MADELINE: *[On the porch, looking back into the doorway of the church.]* You're young. You'll have plenty of time to figure it all out later. In the meantime, just go on and do it.

TAMARA: *[Stepping up from behind DAMARIS to escort her out.]* Might as well, Mare. Everybody's all ready for it. *[Beat.]*

DAMARIS: *[Walks onto the porch.]* Everybody but me.

TAMARA: *[Comes out, closes door. Beat.]*

DAMARIS: *[Grasps MADELINE's arm on the first step down.]* Ma, let me ask you something. What was your baptizing day like? Were you happy? Were you nervous? Tell me about it.

MADELINE: *[Looks away, pulls arm away, clenches the rail, almost caresses the rail, nervously.]* Weren't no big deal, Mare. Your granny had me do it when I was twelve—"the age of accountability," she said.

DAMARIS: Granny HAD you do it?

MADELINE: *[Softly.]* Yeah.

DAMARIS: Did you want to do it?

MADELINE: *[Composed, authoritative tone.]* Damaris, there are certain things expected of a mountain woman. One is to raise her youngins right. Part of that is a-getting them baptized. Come on now, I'll walk most of the way with you. *[The THREE begin to walk slowly down the hill, toward the creek. Parishioners begin singing "Shall We Gather at the River." DAMARIS takes MADELINE's hand, squeezing tightly.]*

DAMARIS: *[Whispers, through clenched teeth.]* Ma, I don't want this.

MADELINE: Smile, Mare. Everybody's looking.

DAMARIS: *[Whispers, through clenched teeth.]* Ma, I'm serious. This ain't right. I'm not ready.

MADELINE: You'll be fine, girl. Suck it up. *[They arrive at the bank of the creek. BROTHER BOYD is in the creek and wades over to meet DAMARIS. He extends a hand. DAMARIS refuses it and steps into the water on her own, then bounds several steps ahead of the preacher.]*

MADELINE: *[Crying softly, hugging herself, talking to God.]* Praise God. Thank you, Jesus. I got one of my baby girls on the right road. Help her, Lord. Bless her, Lord. Let her know how much I love her.

BOYD: Brothers and Sisters, we are gathered here today to witness Damaris' baptism into Christ's church. *[Puts one hand behind DAMARIS' back and the other hand perilously close to her bosom as he gets in position to immerse her.]* In the name of the Father, and of the Son, and of the Holy Gho—

DAMARIS: *[Takes his head and pushes it under, pulling them both down. They both struggle. She is first to her feet; he soon stands. DAMARIS looks at MADELINE.]* I'm sooo sorry, Brother Boyd. I guess I slipped. *[Stomps out of the creek past MADELINE. The congregation begins singing "When the Saved Get to Heaven."]*

[End.]

AUTHOR NOTE *from playwright* DENISE R. MCKINNEY

As a member of the Kentucky Women Playwrights Seminar, I started this play with some trepidation...actually beginning it with characters talking about what happened rather than being in the moment of the action. Playwriting allowed me to step back in my experience, stronger and more resilient, to accomplish a sense of justice, empowerment and good humor. As with most of my writing, it has helped me to heal from woundedness that was deeper than I knew until I began peeling back the layers of self-blame, place, culture, family dynamics and religion. The comic relief found in my sister was a real, true thing, and I wish this for every person in a situation of self-questioning or confusion. *Bless her heart,* as we say in this part of the world. In this instance, it is a compliment and true conferring of deepest thanks.

Stranger on the Porch

Beth Dotson Brown

Characters:
ABBY KANAPPLE   Middle-aged, KEITH's wife of twenty years,
                        an aging beauty
KEITH KANAPPLE   Middle-aged, traveling salesman
EMMA LOWERY   A young woman

Time: 1970s
Place: A midwestern town
Setting: The porch of a middle class house

[At rise, ABBY and KEITH are reading the newspaper on the porch. ABBY looks up from the paper to watch a man, woman and two children walking on the sidewalk.]

ABBY:	There they go again. All five of them.
KEITH:	I only see four.
ABBY:	She's pregnant. In a few months you'll see number five.
	[KEITH returns to his paper. ABBY continues to look after them.]
	I don't understand. We would have made beautiful babies.
KEITH:	*[Puts down newspaper.]* What did you say Abby?
ABBY:	I said we would have made beautiful babies, you and I.
KEITH:	*[Smiles at her.]* You would have made the most precious babies

in the world. It's not like we didn't try.

ABBY: [*Still serious.*] That's not the point, Keith. Why them and not us? We could give a good home to children. And them, well, just look at them!

KEITH: [*Shrugs.*] You would have been a wonderful mother, Abby. I'm sorry we couldn't make it happen. Maybe if I hadn't traveled so much during the first ten years of our marriage. But those days are gone.

ABBY: [*Looks wistfully after the family.*] I would give anything.

KEITH: I have sales calls to make this week on Monday, Tuesday and Wednesday, but if I do well maybe we could take off on Thursday to that lake house of your sister's.

ABBY: That would be lovely.

EMMA: [*Enters wearing a suit and low-heeled, sensible shoes and carrying a case of some sort. She looks at the house number, then addresses them.*] Is this the home of Mr. Keith Kanapple?

KEITH: Yes, ma'am. What can I do for you?

EMMA: You're him? Mr. Kannaple?

ABBY: He is.

EMMA: You don't look at all as I expected. Or as my mother described you. But I supposed it's the distance of years and miles that make it so. [*ABBY and KEITH exchange glances. EMMA puts down her traveling bag and extends a hand, first to ABBY then to KEITH.*] My name is Emma Lowery. At least that's my given name. But I believe that if my mother had followed custom, she would have named me Emma Kanapple.

KEITH: [*Shakes his head and stares.*] What are you trying to tell me?

EMMA: That I believe I'm your daughter. [*KEITH stares at the young woman. ABBY straightens, stopping the movement of the porch swing.*]

ABBY: [*Gapes first at KEITH, then at EMMA.*] You must be, what, nineteen?

EMMA: Oh, no. I'm twenty-one. Rest assured, Mr. Kanapple was acquainted with my mother before he ever met you. And I don't mean to throw a disturbance into your relationship at all. It's just that—[*Looks down demurely at her hands, then to ABBY then KEITH.*] It's just that my mother recently went on to her higher reward and I'm feeling somewhat rootless, having no other siblings, you see. And she always insisted that McGregor Lowrey was my father, but the night he left her I heard him call me her bastard child and since then—

ABBY: Oh, you poor girl. Please sit down. [*Scoots over to give EMMA space on the porch swing. EMMA lightly drops herself onto the swing, barely moving it. ABBY starts to put her arm around the girl's shoulders, but she hesitates and doesn't follow through. KEITH watches the two, shaking his head.]*

ABBY: You must miss your mother terribly.

EMMA: Oh, yes. We were such good friends. The best, really. So, without her, every day is a struggle. That's why I thought that if I could find my father, well, it wouldn't be the same as having Mama back, but it might be something.

KEITH: *[Clears his throat.]* I'm sorry to have to ask, but could you please tell me your mother's name?

EMMA: Marlene. Marlene Knight of Tupelo, Mississippi.

KEITH: Tupelo. I did work Tupelo and nearby for awhile. *[Counts on his fingers, then studies EMMA's face.]*

EMMA: Your name was in her address book from that year, 1952. She got a new one every year and filled them in order, like it was some sort of record of her life, which it sort of is. I didn't see you listed after that.

ABBY: *[Scowls at KEITH, then turns lovingly to EMMA.]* Do you still live in Tupelo, Emma?

EMMA: Oh, I've been traveling around somewhat, educating myself about the world I guess you could say.

KEITH: How so?

EMMA: *[Speaks a very southern, storytelling cadence.]* Well, even though I didn't know my real father's family, I was well-acquainted with mother's family—six sisters and one brother. Most of them live in Tupelo still to this day, but Aunt Susie and Aunt Renny both moved to Mobile, Alabama. And the baby, Uncle Jacob, he settled near Memphis. He has a real sweet wife, Melody, who loves it when I come to stay. Unlike my aunts, she didn't grow up with sisters, and since she and Uncle Jacob only have boys, at least so far, Melody just loves to have another girl around.

ABBY: That's lovely that you have your family, but it doesn't make up for not having parents, does it? *[EMMA'S eyes drop to study her shoes. She puts her elbows on her knees and drops her face into them, as if crying.]*

ABBY: *[Moves closer to encircle the girl with her arm. Speaks quietly.]* Have you eaten anything? I could fix you a sandwich now if you're hungry. Or you could join us later for supper. I'm making Keith's favorite, pot roast. *[Glances over at KEITH. He stares blankly at the two women.]*

EMMA: *[Sits up slowly, wipes her cheeks dry of any tears she might have shed. Looks at KEITH.]* Would you mind very much if I stay for supper?

ABBY: Of course he won't mind, dear.

KEITH: Abby, isn't it time for you to start cooking? My stomach is beginning to growl.

ABBY: *[Looks at EMMA as if afraid to leave her.]* But this is such a good time to get acquainted, for all three of us. *[Smiles at EMMA, appears to be very happy.]* Tell us more about yourself.

EMMA: Well, I rode the bus here. It was a long ride, but without a car it was my only option. And, as I'm sure you know, the bus station is a fair piece from your home, so it was a little walk.

ABBY: But you really wanted to find us.

EMMA: Oh, yes, I most certainly did.

KEITH: Abby, could you get me some iced tea. And I'm sure our guest would like some, also.

ABBY: *[Still unsure about leaving them.]* I'll hurry and be right back. *[Exits. EMMA watches KEITH. She begins to push the swing lightly, and its creaking fills the porch.]*

KEITH: I've sold a lot of things to a lot of people during my life. I went door-to-door with encyclopedias, vacuum cleaners and household cleaning products. Every one had some beneficial trait that would make the buyer happy.

EMMA: So you're a salesman?

KEITH: Born that way, I suspect. Sometimes traits are passed on from father to daughter.

EMMA: Sometimes.

KEITH: *[Gets up and walks to the far corner of the porch, counting on his fingers again.]* What did you say your mother's name was?

EMMA: Marlene Knight.

KEITH: Did she ever call herself Marly?

EMMA: Why, yes, she did. Aunt Susie still refers to her as Marly.

KEITH: *[Shakes his head in remembrance.]* Yes, you do have a family resemblance. And your voice, the way you talk, it's just like her.

EMMA: So you do remember!

KEITH: I remember Marly. I remember a fun-loving, pretty little gal who talked a mile a minute to me about how she knew Hank Williams even before he got famous. That did impress me for some reason. *[Appears to be searching his memory, then speaks as if to himself.]* Marly Knight and I had a baby.

EMMA: You had a baby but now you have a grown daughter.

KEITH: *[Speaks in an accusing tone.]* Why me? There must be other names in the book that you could check.

EMMA: *[Appears hurt.]* There are dates. The dates by your name make the most sense. They fit.

KEITH: *[Pauses and considers her from across the porch.]* What is it that you want, Ms. Lowery? I'm sure you came here for a reason.

EMMA: *[Furrows her brow.]* I came to meet my father.

KEITH:	What's your birth date, Ms. Lowery?
EMMA:	August 27, 1952.
KEITH:	*[Paces the porch.]* August. My first visit to Tupelo was earlier that year, maybe February. Then I went back in, let me see, I believe it was July. I saw Marly again then—dancing outside at the drive-in with some girlfriends. She wore a summer sweater that looked mighty fine on her little figure. *[Turns directly toward EMMA.]* The dates might fit, but either Marly wasn't your mother or you were born later. I saw her in July and her stomach wasn't sheltering a baby. *[EMMA locks eyes with him, as if challenging him to go on.]* I'll ask you again. What is it you want?
EMMA:	It works all the time in the storybooks. Anne of Green Gables. That lost girl that Audrey Hepburn played in Breakfast at Tiffany's. Someone always takes them in and gives them something they've never had before, making their life better and more exciting.
KEITH:	What have you never had that you're looking for?
EMMA:	*[Drops her eyes to her feet, them slowly raises them back to KEITH.]* A father.
KEITH:	*[Looks away from her out toward the sidewalk while EMMA gazes at him hopefully. KEITH turns back to her.]* How about a mother?
EMMA:	Oh, your wife is nice and all, but I don't need her. I learned from my mother that it's the man who holds the wallet.
KEITH:	*[Angrily]* You are the worst kind of liar. You're not just trying to get money, you're dealing with hearts here. *[Takes his wallet out of his back pocket, pulls out cash and hands it to her.]* Take this and get out of here. And don't come back. *[ABBY comes back onto the porch with two iced teas.]*
EMMA:	*[Snatches the money, folds it in half then stuffs it in her jacket pocket as she stands up.]* I was looking forward to that pot roast.
KEITH:	Abby makes a good pot roast, with fresh meat and vegetables, none of that fake stuff they try to sell you in packages in the grocery story. Abby is the real deal on everything. *[EMMA nods, picks up her case then walks past KEITH.]* Maybe you'll learn to be the real deal some day.
EMMA:	*[Stops and turns to look back at ABBY.]* I guess you can have my iced tea. *[Exits. ABBY puts the tea glasses on the table next to KEITH, who returns to his seat. ABBY stands, dumbstruck.]*
KEITH:	Please, Abby, sit down. *[ABBY returns to her spot on the swing and looks fondly at the spot where EMMA sat.]* She wasn't my daughter, Abby.
ABBY:	But...but...the girl doesn't have any family, Keith. And

	neither do we.
KEITH:	It's for the best, Abby.
ABBY:	She doesn't have anyone. We could have at least given her a good, hot meal. *[KEITH shakes his head as if worried. Goes to sit next to ABBY, who sobs quietly.]* For a moment, I could just see us all together. You and I and our daughter, going to church on Christmas day, unwrapping gifts from under the tree, drinking hot chocolate together. Like a real family.
KEITH:	*[Gently places his palm over his wife's hand.]* We are a family already, dear. I couldn't want anything more than you.
ABBY:	But I could, Keith. And I almost had it.
KEITH:	Abby, she's not my daughter.
ABBY:	But she could have been. Could have been mine, too. Didn't you always tell me that salesmen know how to twist someone's fantasy into a truth?
KEITH:	I don't think twisting a little fantasy into a tiny truth is the same as creating a family based on a lie. Besides, that girl was so slick that I wouldn't doubt if her mother is alive and breathing happily as she sends her out on these visits to raise money for the family.
ABBY:	How can you say something so vile about a person as sweet as that? *[Looks out toward the sidewalk.]* There must be something she really needs, some hole in her heart that she's trying to fill. *[ABBY and KEITH rock on the swing in silence as ABBY continues to watch the sidewalk. Sees the family come into view again.]* There they go again. Maybe they would like some iced tea or something to eat. *[Gets up and begins to walk out toward them.]*
EMMA:	*[On the other side of the set, EMMA is knocking on a door.]* My name is Emma Lowery. At least that's my given name. But I believe that if my mother had followed custom, she would have named me Emma McClinton.

[End.]

Author Note *from playwright* Beth Dotson Brown

Sitting on the front porch of our more than 100-year-old house provides a unique view of life in small town Kentucky. Because of the raspberry bushes and the slight rise of our yard next to the sidewalk, walkers rarely glance downward to see anyone on the porch. That leaves me to study those characters and let their stories speak to me.

One day as I pondered the con artists I had met throughout my life, and previous families who might have lived in our house, these characters came together. "The Stranger on the Porch" emerged. This play considers how far people might be able to carry a con when greed, hope and doubt collide. Perhaps it's possible for the right lie to be just what these characters want. In this play, childless Abby embraces Emma when she shows up on the front porch claiming to be her husband's daughter. But is she?

This play is available for performance through www.heartlandplays.com.

excerpt from

The Gifts of the Spirit

BELINDA MASON

Time:	Present
Place:	Rural Kentucky
Setting:	A small funeral home. Folding chairs randomly arranged. A "kitchen" room offstage to left where food is taken. A small room offstage to right where the immediate family is sequestered. A casket and floral arrangements at the right of the stage. A pink floor lamp stands at each end of the casket, and a podium is nearby.

[The characters have gathered for the wake of a young man who has died in a car wreck. They are some of the members of a close-knit community. They speak casually and, for the most part, comfortably to one another. The atmosphere is fairly informal, though subdued, and they are free to move about, to view the body or to arrange themselves in different groupings.]

Scene V – Enoch

PREACHER: And among the gifts is faith.

ENOCH: A man's born without a thing and he dies that self-same way. So he's got to make the most of what's in the middle. Now, they's plenty of 'em that would fault me on this, but if the good Lord hadn't a-meant for us to enjoy life, he'd a-took us straight to heaven when we was born and skipped over it.

And look a-here at what all he's give us:

>Children.

>Fishin'.

>Dogwood trees.

>Pie.

Them might not be yore picks, but they's mine. They's plenty other fine things. But git ye head out of ye hind end for a minute and think about it.

>Music.

>Buddies.

>Biscuit.

Now, I'm not what you'd call a religious man, for I believe religion ain't necessarily limited to the church house. Don't git me wrong, though, the church house is good for a lot. When I was a young man, I did a-sight of courtin' at meetings. And in the middle of my years, sometimes there wasn't a thing in the world that was any better than cleanin' up, walkin' down the creek with Virgie and the younguns, and listenin' to some preachin'. Set on them satiny-smooth benches, spring of the year coming in the winders, and the smell of them talcum powders when Virgie'd git that fan goin'.

Brother Felix Ison'ud get wound up. They used to say he preached starvation instead of salvation. I'd listen to him a while, then take note of everybody. My neighbors, I'd think to myself. My fam'ly. My friends. Lord, hit was sweet. A good feelin'. Then maybe I'd put my arm around Virgie and squeeze that soft part of her betwixt the shoulder and elbow. My hands is old now, but they remember yet holdin' that woman's skin.

I've studied on it, and I believe now what I loved so good about them times is how all of us fit together. As tight and true as a dove-tail joint. Musta been somethin' to it, for they was certain days in church I even loved my mother-in-law.

Now, the truth is that Mag Muncy was a bitch. She worked her husband to death and then set in on her younguns. Cold as ice, that woman. Virgie was her oldest, and Mag done her like a pack horse. 'Course she never could forgive me for takin' her. But here I'd set, in back of Mag, filled with somethin' that coulda been the Holy Ghost for all I know about such matters, and they'd be ten-minute spaces of time when I loved Mag. Loved how straight she sat, like she had a poker up her rear. Loved them stingy little plaits around her head. Not seein' her old mouth, nothin' but a line across her face, but lovin' that, too.

But what I meant to say is that they's a lot of 'em that wouldn't pick me for a religious man. I handle back talk. I'll take a drank. And I ain't never been baptized.

Virgie's accused me more'n once of blasphemin'.

Years ago I had Frank Fulton helpin' me clear a spot of ground up in Sandlick
Gap. Wadn't nothing up there but a wilderness. We'd work our
asses off. Cuttin' trees, burnin' brash, grubbin' roots. People
thought I'd gone crazy, and some said as much. But I knowed
underneath all them woods was a fine little house seat. Long
about August, it started to shape up, and hit was so purty I
decided I'd build a house for myself.

Little Ted Adams, he was the Presbyterian preacher, he was from off somewhere,
he come by one day and was braggin' and goin' on. I had the
footer poured and was fixin' to lay the foundation. You could
already see what a fine dwellin' house I was gonna have. Little
Ted said, 'Now, just think, Enoch. All this belongs to you and
the Lord.' I said, 'Well, preacher. You shoulda seen it when the
Lord owned it by hisself.' Frank Fulton, he's dead now, told
that all over the country.

Now, I'm a carpenter and Jesus was, too. And I know if he was any hand at all,
he paid mind to how things fits together. If a man's gonna
build for it to stand, they's certain things he's got to believe
in. You got to believe in the level. You got to have faith in the
chalk-line. You have to trust the square.

Workin' on a buildin' is what livin' is. And just like good workin', you've got to
have things to believe in before you can build somethin' that'll
stand. A house that'll keep the wind off of ye. A life where the
doors is hung right and the roof don't bow.

And like I said at the outset, the Lord's give us plenty to delight in and a whole
lot to believe. If they is a day of judgment comin', as some says,
I don't think we'll be faulted much for drankin' or gamblin' nor
none of the other things you heard is a one-way ticket to hell.
If he's got a quarrel with us, it'll be for us not layin' hold of our
tools. Not trustin' our materials.

I'm an old man and I figure now it don't matter so much what you believe.

So long as you believe somethin'.

> The Democrat party.
> A good huntin' dog.
> General Motors products.
> The UMW.
> They's plenty to pick from.
>   *[End.]*

INFORMATIONAL NOTE *about playwright* BELINDA MASON

This excerpt from the play *The Gifts of the Spirit*
is contained in the Belinda Mason Papers,
1997MS348, Special Collections and Digital Programs,
University of Kentucky Libraries,
and is used with permission of Stephen Carden,
executor of the literary estate of Belinda Mason.

excerpts from

The Way Home
a spoken opera

Constance Alexander

Characters:

THERESA FLOWERS	50, a woman with a life-threatening illness
REPORTER	50s, a writer who interviews THERESA
CHORUS	2-4 people of any age, mostly female

Time:	Present day
Place:	Rural area of Trigg County, Kentucky
Setting:	A rented mobile home

[Following are four excerpts that feature THERESA. The first covers the initial interview with the REPORTER at THERESA's trailer. In the second, THERESA is well into treatment. In the third excerpt, her tumor marker level has increased and a new, very expensive therapy is prescribed, which sparks an inspiring dream. The fourth scene describes the end of the project.]

Excerpt 1

THERESA: Turn right,
             right after the lake.
             Follow that road.

REPORTER: Past junked cars,
     rusted-out school buses,
     a quarry, the sign
     for an old church
     that burned down.

THERESA: When you get to the creek,
     turn left.
     You're there when you get
     to the mailbox with flowers
     on it.
     Right here.

REPORTER: Let's see.
     Tape recorder.
     Batteries.
     Notebook.
     Pen. Not that one.
     I've got to get
     a better notebook.
     Not today.

THERESA: I've been listening for you.
     For the car.

REPORTER: Your directions were great.
     Didn't get lost once, but
     I never actually saw the quarry.

CHORUS: She stands on the porch of her trailer;
     hugs herself against the chill.
     The scarf wrapped around her head is splashed
     with purple, fuchsia and rivers
     of green. Her hands flutter to straighten
     the scarf, to check the swell of its silken knot
     and the tucked-in tails.

THERESA: I washed my hair today and a lot of it fell out.
     When I came outside to dry my head off,
     the rest of it went.

CHORUS: The autumn colors have faded to rust.
     The sedge grass is bleached blond.

THERESA: The leaves are falling and my hair's falling out.
     So I thought, well, that's okay. In the spring,
     the leaves will all come back
     and so will my hair.
     It's kind of like that. Life's
     like that sometimes.
     Come on in.

CHORUS: Afternoon sun slants through the lace curtains.

On the kitchen table, a bowl of plums.
Sleek purple orbs, smooth as gigolos.
The cloth, handmade, is from Budapest,
embroidered with blue and white flowers.

REPORTER: My favorite color. Blue.
Hmmm. What smells so good?

THERESA: I made tea and baked muffins.
The smell of the muffins reminds me that
I want my mother. Not my real mother,
but the mother I wish I had,
who could keep me safe
and read me stories until
I fall asleep.
I can feel her hand, gentle and cool on my forehead,
checking for fever.

Excerpt 2

CHORUS: You wait till they call your name
at the Four Rivers
Cancer Center.
The chairs are lined up like a firing squad.
Stiff, gray plastic.
A Coke machine hums its single note
until someone actually buys one.
One, two, three, four
quarters and then the thud of the can
dropping. It could be a gunshot,
the way we all jump.

REPORTER: So, what's it like? Chemotherapy.

THERESA: You have to take steroids and
Tagamet before.
It makes your bones hurt
but they say it's good for you.
When they call you, it's time
to go into the room.
There's a whole bunch of people together.
Hooked up to tubes.

REPORTER: A group? You're not alone?
Do you read, or take notes? What?

THERESA: We sit in a circle like Girl Scouts.
We talk a lot because of the steroids
we take the night before.
Only thing I can read
during chemo

is Louis L'Amour.
I love the cheap hotels, the gun fights,
a new marshal comes to town to kick butt.

CHORUS: Utah Blaine. El Paso.
I come to rout this town
of the varmint that's stealing horses
and robbin' banks.
It ain't right. Losing three marshals
in three months.
I stopped cattle rustlin' up north,
train robberies out west.
You think I can't clean up this town?
His spurs make as much noise as tap dancer shoes,
but he's no sissy, even tho' he tips his hat
to the ladies and says yes ma'am and no ma'am
like some mealy-mouth mama's boy.
He's rangy, raw-boned, squinty-eyed
but not in a shifty way,
if ya know what I mean.
It's from riding into all them sunsets.
When he pushes the doors of the saloon open
the place gets all quiet like,
and the bartender starts polishin' clean glasses
with a dirty towel and dartin' looks into the mirror.
The guys playin' poker push away from the table in back.
And the chorus girls sneak upstairs so they don't
get their feathers blown off in a gunfight or nothin'.
Utah's faster on the draw than the outlaw,
but he don't kill him. He takes him in and waits
for the judge to come to town
'cause that's the way justice works.
No lynchin' on my watch. We do things legal-like.
The hangin' judge'll be here 'fore the next new moon.

Excerpt 3

REPORTER: What's it like living out here
all by yourself?

THERESA: You don't know how your body is going to react
when you start a new treatment.
So being alone is another kind of a scary thing.
I got pretty sick the other night,
here by myself. It was right
in the middle of the night,
but I made it through.

	Sometimes you just don't know.
REPORTER:	So. Any dreams?
THERESA:	Oh, gosh.

My girlfriend was so anxious to find out
if I made it through my second night
of the new chemo, and I was just totally sound asleep
and I was having this dream.
I was in this great big complex of shops
that sold different art materials and gifts
and unusual clothing and other items.
All handmade.
And I was just walking through and thinking,
"How pretty."
I couldn't afford any of it,
but I was just enjoying it all.
And I was supposed to be meeting some friends,
but I couldn't find anybody.
And then I couldn't find my truck.
I was lost
and it was getting dark.
And then someone tapped me
on the shoulder.
I turned around
and saw this angel with a great big
pink fluffy sweater on,
pink chenille.
And she crooked her finger at me,
like, Come on. Follow me.
So I went with her up this hill
and there was this big warehouse
with stained glass windows.
All these people had great big pieces of cloth spread out
on the floor
and they were painting. The idea was to take a roller
and make your own pictures.
So I was just beginning to paint and thinking,
"This has got some possibilities..."
And then the phone rang and it was my friend,
seeing if I made it through the night.

REPORTER:	So you got what you needed.
THERESA:	Yeah. What I like best,

is when you think positively
there are people along the way
to help you find your way

through the confusion.
Just like my friends,
and the pharmacist.
I never thought I would get help like this.
I never expected it. I was so amazed
when the pharmacist's wife called
to say her husband
had ordered the medicine.

CHORUS: It will be here tomorrow
and you can start taking it.

THERESA: I just felt like that
was a miracle.
There are people along the way
that say, "Come this way.
There are ways
through all this."
You just have to keep believing positively
and really miraculous things can develop.
Your way becomes clear.

Excerpt 4

REPORTER: I still haven't told Theresa that Pat died,
but she never asks about her anymore either.
This end-of-life project is officially over now.
The funding has run out and I have to
go on to something new.
But I have boxes of files.
Transcripts from scores of interviews.
And these stories. These voices.
Some people tell me I should write a book about it.
Others say it's all too depressing
and wonder what's wrong with me.

CHORUS: Write a comedy. A musical.
What's wrong with something light
for a change?

REPORTER: They want to know if I've changed,
doing all this death-and-dying stuff.

CHORUS: And you say—?

REPORTER: I finally changed the beneficiary on my life insurance
so my first husband won't get a penny.
I have a living will.
And when I die—note that I said "when," not "if"—
I'm going to be cremated and have the ashes scattered
off the Brooklyn Bridge.

My funeral service is planned.
Right down to the music.
Including the whole album of
Sergeant Pepper's Lonely Hearts Club Band.
I'd tell you more, but I'm out of time.
I have to go get Theresa.
She's at chemo today
and she needs a way home.

[End.]

AUTHOR NOTE *from playwright* CONSTANCE ALEXANDER

As independent producer of *Promises to Keep*, a radio series
on end-of-life issues, I conducted scores of interviews.
Two women—both of them fighting cancer—participated throughout
the course of the documentary series, and they inspired *The Way Home*.

The woman called Theresa Flowers in the script had been treated for
breast cancer in 1988. Thirteen years later, when she was diagnosed with
ovarian cancer, she was uninsured because she could not afford the high
premiums demanded of cancer survivors. At around the same time,
her long-term partner abandoned the relationship because
the second bout with cancer was "too much" for him.
As a result, Theresa lost her home and her business,
and ended up renting a trailer in a rural part of Trigg County.

Articles and radio pieces featuring Theresa compelled a Calloway County
woman named Pat (who was fighting stage IV breast cancer)
to donate $1,000 to help with Theresa's medical bills.
Over time, the Theresa Fund raised nearly $8,000.

The Way Home weaves the stories of Pat and Theresa together in a form
I call a "spoken opera." Written in free verse, it has operatic qualities—
arias, duets, a chorus. Designed for readers theatre, the text is read rather
than memorized, thus allowing performances by actors with a range of
abilities and ages, and providing flexibility in terms of performance space,
blocking, lighting and other technical concerns.

After the first staged reading at Horse Cave Theater,
The Way Home has been performed in Arkansas, California, Georgia,
Illinois, multiple Kentucky locations, Louisiana,
Massachusetts, New York and New Jersey.
Groups that produce *The Way Home* use it without any
royalties to the playwright, as long as funds raised from performances
are donated to hospice, the uninsured, breast cancer,
or other related causes.

excerpt from

The Honey Harvest

Liz Fentress

Characters:
MELISSA HOLT   Mid-20s, single woman
P.J. TRUE   Mid-20s, MELISSA's childhood friend

Time: Present day, an evening in September
Place: Outskirts of a small town in western Wisconsin
Setting: Behind a modest house—a beehive stands at the edge
of the yard

[MELISSA has dropped out of college to care for her father who suffers from depression. At summer's end, she talks to a childhood friend, P.J., about beekeeping.]

[Act II, Scene ii]
MELISSA: You know, you think you know what's goin' on—but you don't.
Remember this summer, when I got stung so bad?
P.J.:   Your hand was swoll up like a cauliflower.
MELISSA: I wanted to find the queen. You know, check on her. And I always
try to make working with the bees a positive experience. Like I
decide in advance to have a positive attitude. So I put my stuff on
and said, "This is gonna be a positive experience." And I opened the

hive. But the bees started freaking out right away, and it didn't seem like they wanted someone messing around with their lives. I mean they were buzzing around my veil—like, attacking me.

Then I started feeling pricks on my hands; the bees were pricking me through my gloves. I thought, "They're pricking me, but they can't be stinging me." I had my head so set it was a positive experience that I didn't believe the bees were stinging me.

I went through the deep hive bodies looking for the queen. But the bees kept pricking me and it made me mad which made me jerk the equipment around which probably made them madder.

I kept thinking, "This is positive, damn it. The bees cannot make this into any other kind of experience."

You know, when a bee stings you, its stinger comes out and it dies. Well, I noticed all these stingers in my gloves. My gloves were covered with stingers and my hands were hurting. But I still wouldn't admit the bees were stinging me! I thought, "Look at all the stingers in my gloves. You'd think the bees were stinging me because my hands hurt, too, but they're not! I'm having a positive experience, damn it!"

Finally, I mean, my hands were throbbing, it occurred to me the bees WERE stinging me. And it was not a positive experience! It was awful! So I gave up. Quit. Quit before I found the queen. Put the hive together and went back to the house and felt like shit. Because I set out to do something and failed.

P.J.:   I don't get it.

MELISSA: Here's my point, P.J. You don't know what's in the hive. It doesn't matter what you're doing, you shouldn't start by saying, "This is gonna be a good experience." Because it might not be. The bees could have lost their queen, or they might have a disease, or they might not like the weather. And if the bees are feeling mean, well, then, going into the hive is not going to be a positive experience, no matter how hard you try. You don't know what's in the hive. Remember that. You don't know what's in the hive.

[End.]

AUTHOR NOTE *from playwright* LIZ FENTRESS

When I was a child, my mom bought big jars of honey from a Czech woman we called the Honey Lady. One day the Honey Lady said, "The bees sing to me. I know when times are good—because the bees sing." That experience, lodged in a far-away corner of my mind, became the germinal idea for my play *The Honey Harvest*.

Thirty-five years later, on a beautiful Derby Day morning, I picked up my first order of package bees at the Middletown post office. I would soon have many beekeeping stories of my own to draw on for a play.

At a beekeeping conference in Midway that summer, I learned that there are more books about bees than any other subject except God. The two I used most while doing research for *The Honey Harvest* are *The Dancing Bees* by Karl von Frisch and *The Sacred Bee* by Hilda Ransome.

I found the time and space to write *The Honey Harvest* during day retreats at Hopscotch House, a retreat program of the Kentucky Foundation for Women. The play was developed in Horse Cave through the Kentucky Voices program. Following a staged reading, Robert Brock said he'd produce it at Kentucky Repertory Theatre. Many thanks to Robert, and to Julie Crutcher who served as dramaturg for that experience.

Because someone once told me, "It's a draft until you die," I continued to work on *The Honey Harvest* the following year with dramaturg Liz Engelman at The Playwrights Center in Minneapolis. The revised script won the North American Actors Association Playwriting Competition and was staged at the Tristan Bates Theatre in London's West End.

I'm working on a new play now, but I still keep bees—and they're singing.

The Fish in the Dumpster

Nancy Gall-Clayton

Characters:
ANGIE   20s or early 30s, alone

Time: Present, late fall, 2 a.m.
Place: Rural Kansas
Setting: Outside a gas station off an expressway exit

ANGIE: *[Touching her belly.]* It was a flip-floppy fish-sort-of feeling, mostly
          right around my belly button—strong sometimes, like one of them
          orange fishes flinging itself upstream on nature shows you see on TV.
I thought I might be able to kill the thing if I drunk a whole bunch of liquid—
          not alcohol, I don't care for the taste and I didn't want to pickle it—but
          water so cold it would sting my teeth—and apple juice and Kool-Aid—
          healthy drinks, things they give kids in daycare, things to shock it.
And if I couldn't kill it while it was IN me, I planned to squeeze it OUT OF
          ME by filling up my belly with more food than I could hold, like how
          water spills over the edge of the tub when you run it too long and you
          step in and something has to give. I wish I could tell Jimmy it worked.
He was real nice, Jimmy. IS nice, I should say. Winter was coming when we met,
          and he bought me a coat right off. It had one of them fake fur collars
          that feel nice and warm and smooth up against your cheek.

Jimmy and me, we met by the Krispy Kreme doughnut case at a Pilot station
somewheres in Ohio. I was drinking coffee with lots of that Amaretta
flavoring in it. That's the one in the purple container. Gee, I could drink
that stuff straight! Actually, I do sometimes.

Anyways, there I was, kinda leaning on the doughnut case, getting ready to take
a sip of coffee, and he walks in and smiles at me, like he knows some
secret, a good secret I mean, and he looks smack dab into my eyes.
Something—Fate, I guess you might call it—makes me toast him. I was
loving his gold tooth with the heart cut-out, too, so I hold up my coffee
cup and say, "Cheers!" like we was old pals celebrating some important
occasion, maybe a tenth wedding anniversary. He sees right off I have
class, little more knowledge than the usual lady you see at a truck stop.

"Hold that," he says and swats me on the bottom and walks off in the direction
of the men's room. "Hold what?" I'm thinking to myself. "Hold what?
The coffee? The way I'm standing? Something he meant to hand me?"

When he comes back out, he smiles again, and the sunlight kinda bounces off
that gold heart on his tooth. He bumps his leg smack into mine—
accidentally on purpose. "You with someone?" he asks.

"You," I say, deciding on the spot. "You, if that's your eighteen-wheeler out
there."

The night I met him I looked REAL fine, but then I am the kind that flowers
after midnight. My hair was tied back, white-blonde I think it was then,
and I had me an almost-new pair of hiking boots with rawhide laces so
long they went 'round my ankles twice. My roomie at the shelter give
'em to me 'cause they pinched her toes.

Jimmy must have liked the way I was looking 'cause he said, "Follow me," and
we was on our way to Oklahoma with a load of bikes. Said he delivered
them all over. I didn't know kids rode bikes so much. Me, I was twelve
the last time I was on one and racing like crazy to get away from a mean
dog that actually bit into my rear end. The sheriff come out and said I
should pull down my pants and let him take a look at the bite, but my
dad said no and he'd call if I started acting like I had rabies.

Almost as soon as I get in the truck, Jimmy asks me if I have any dreams, so I
know that he is a quality-type person. I decide to show him I'm one,
too, and ask him to go first. His dream is to drive cross-country in a
truck carrying three layers of brand new cars. Three layers, like one of
them wedding cakes rich people have. He wants to climb into the very
highest car, smoke Marlboros, and watch the sky when the stars are
shooting around. I ain't never seen shooting stars myself, but Jimmy
has. He got so caught up telling me 'bout his dream, he forgot to ask
for mine, but that was okay.

The back of Jimmy's truck is real nice, with a mattress, three pillows, a big ol'
fluffy quilt from Tennessee, and a wooden box to put things in. Glued
on one end of the box is a picture of a tall, thin dancing lady wearing

a hat with fruit all over it, looking like she could click her high heels and dance and sing all at once. Everything about the fruit-hat lady is stretched out, like she was once one of those long, thin babies with the long fingers that make everybody say, "She's going to be a piano player," even if no one in the family knows the difference between the white keys and the pedals. When I was in Vacation Bible School, I asked the minister why the song didn't get no faster when the lady pressed on the pedals, and he wouldn't tell me. It's like a secret piano players have, I guess. I only got to go to that Vacation Bible School just the one summer when I stayed up to Gram's 'cause dad was off doing construction, and mom was in jail on account of writing too many bad checks.

It was cozy snuggling with Jimmy in the back of that truck. I loved it when he'd fling his long legs over me like he was trying to protect me from something evil. He couldn't, of course, because the evil thing was IN me. I think it was June when it began flipping around so fierce-like.

Living in a truck, your days run together kinda like fence posts out here in Kansas, and it might not of been June. I couldn't keep up with the time of day neither 'cause my watch was missing the hour hand. Fell off for some reason. It's still in there though… See? *[Points, shakes the arm with the watch.]* When you press down on both buttons, it makes a green glow. I pretend the green opens into a magic world where pixies live. I might still believe in pixies.

Anyways, it was fall when Jimmy told me he didn't like fat women. Had to be fall 'cause school buses were suddenly everywhere. I was fat all right— my belly was almost full enough to flood the fish out, but Jimmy didn't want to wait, I guess. Elsewise, he never would have left me at this here gas station last week. Or maybe he was mad 'cause I spent too long in the ladies room talking to the fish. When I finally come out, I got me a couple extra Amarettas and he says, "Come on, Angie. I'm gonna be late." I never did hear him worrying about being late 'fore that night.

I got in the truck and we was about to drive out of this here very parking lot when Jimmy stops real sudden-like and hands me a Ben Franklin.

"Hon," he says, sounding kinda sweet and more like himself again, "Go in and get me a pack of Marlboros."

"You know they won't take that this time of night," I says, trying real hard to think about the fruit-hat lady to take my mind off my belly pains.

"Here," he says, taking Ben back and handing me two twenties. Now that there should have been a big enough clue, giving me TWO bills and all, but I wasn't thinking too clear. When I come out with the Marlboros, the truck is gone. Just plain gone. I stare real hard in every direction and then I go walking down *[Points.]* that little road over there. Guess what's down there? A WELFARE OFFICE. I've been trying to puzzle out if Jimmy knew it was there, if he planned this, but I'm doubting it. I won't be talking to no social worker, leastwise not till first frost. I sure didn't have time to talk to one that night. That last sip of coffee musta done it. About the time I get back from my walk and go over *[Points.]* to that pump, no, *[Points in another direction.]* that diesel pump, it was, trying to spot the 18-wheeler, water starts gushing from between my legs. That fish starts talking and tells me to go back in them woods *[Points.]* behind the dumpster, back there up the hill a little. And off I go. Guess what's leaning on the dumpster—a long box with a picture of a shiny red bike on it! And a bike in it, too.

I move the box to the back of the dumpster and make a wall so nobody can bother me while I'm pushing out my fish. The woods is stretching out behind and over my head, stars are twinkling down. The building looks real bright against the darkness, and I can hear cars and trucks whoosh-ing by every so often while I'm pushing.

After a whole lot of commotion in my belly, that fish finally swims outa me and lands on a pile of wet leaves. It's slimy and slick when I try to pick it up, and its tail is still attached to something up inside me. Luckily, I find a tin can lid so I hack at the tail, and it finally came off. I cut my hand. Not a big cut—here, see. *[Shows her cut.]*

Anyway I'm noticing newspapers stacked up beside the dumpster. I tell myself I should wrap up the fish in a newspaper and I do. It flops around for a minute—and even makes a little whimpering sound. I ignore every-thing and just fling the whole mess into the dumpster. "Good-bye, Amaretta," I say, "and good riddance." Probably shouldn'ta give it the name of something I like, but it was all I could think of at the time. It landed near a big ol' mound of coffee grounds.

Then I pressed them buttons on my watch and thought about magic and pixies. I spread out the coat Jimmy got me at the Salvation Army, and I lay me down to sleep just like that prayer.

That was five days ago, I think, four or five. Yesterday a giant truck come along and backed up to the dumpster and hauled the whole thing off. I guess the fish is in a landfill somewheres by now and can't bother nobody. I 'spect Jimmy will be glad to know that. I'm figuring he'll be stopping off on his way back to Ohio. He left me a bike and give me money. That means he cares about me, and he's coming back, you know? He only left 'cause he was gonna be late for something.

And that's why I'm sleeping in the woods and just coming in for snacks and the bathroom after midnight, like now. If I go off somewhere, he won't have no way to find me. Yeah, Jimmy, he'll be back real soon, so, no, mister, thanks all the same, but I really can't go off with you. *[Pause.]* I don't mind talking a spell longer though. And, oh! I just remembered: I've got that pack of Marlboros I bought for Jimmy. They're down in this pocket next to my Amarettas. Would you care for a smoke?

[End.]

AUTHOR NOTE *from playwright* NANCY GALL-CLAYTON

I've always been fascinated by the mysteries and theories
surrounding birth and a mother's instincts.
My dog knew exactly what to do as I, an amazed 10-year-old,
watched her deliver four puppies, lick them clean, and nurse.
Some years later, my cat also was doing what nature dictated
when she ate one of her kittens. The kitten may have been malformed
or the litter size may have overwhelmed the cat.

At times, humans, too, may be hot-wired to kill newborns that they or
their communities cannot accept. Killing infants was a common practice
among many ancient civilizations, and today, thirty countries provide a
special defense for mothers who commit neonaticide.
Some women who kill their newborns have not acknowledged their
pregnancies—even to themselves. Others who know they are pregnant
but realize neither motherhood nor adoption is feasible choose abortion.

If life is mostly a straight line, awakenings and experiences that
keep it from being perfectly straight for me include the following:
learning that a classmate's "older sister" was her mother,
a sister's pregnancy at 17, a friend's sterility from an illegal abortion,
volunteering with the Problem Pregnancy and Abortion Counseling
Project (detailed in *Standing Up for Reproductive Rights:
The Struggle for Legal Abortion in Kentucky*),
working in the family planning clinic at Louisville General Hospital
where I met a 36-year-old grandmother, earning a law degree at age 30
that led to assisting Rep. Gerta Bendl make Kentucky's laws
gender neutral, being part of the team that revised the Juvenile Code,
and representing in Family Court children
alleged to be abused and neglected.

Another milestone experience for me was
giving birth to twin boys at age 38, a joy and continuing blessing.

My play was inspired by those women for whom pregnancy and birth
are neither joy nor blessing. I wish them well.

Ward 101

Gail Livesay

Characters:
BRENDA   Middle-aged, patient in a psychiatric ward
HERBIE   BRENDA's imaginary friend
NURSE BB   50s, the duty nurse

Time: Present
Place: A city
Setting: Hospital patient lounge, BRENDA's room, nurses' station

[Patient lounge with magazines, newspapers and paper cups strewn about, perhaps a cot to indicate BRENDA's room, something that resembles a linen closet and a nurse's station. The different areas could be indicated by simple lighting changes.]

HERBIE: I bet that nurse is CORN FED. *[Beat.]* Ask her.
BRENDA: Are you corn fed?
NURSE BB: Are you trying to be smart with me?
HERBIE: People with the most beautiful skin eat a lot of corn.
BRENDA: Corn makes the skin beautiful.
NURSE BB: Why thank you, Brenda.
HERBIE: Can I sing your favorite song, Boot Scootin' Boogie?
BRENDA: Don't you dare.

NURSE BB:	I think it's time for your medicine.
HERBIE:	It will make you sleep or be zombiefied.
BRENDA:	I won't take it!
NURSE BB:	I'll stand here all day if I have to. *[Beat.]* Open your mouth and stick out your tongue and let me see your hand. *[Gives BRENDA medicine, which BRENDA pretends to take. NURSE BB exits.]*
HERBIE:	You'd think she'd be smart enough to look in the other hand.
BRENDA:	I'm going to the lounge and see if someone will talk to me.
HERBIE:	What am I, chopped liver?
BRENDA:	If I socialize, the nurse will think the medicine I didn't take is making me feel better. *[Crosses to lounge and mimes talking to somebody.]* Hi. I'm not sick. Mom and Dad just wanted to vacation without me and gave me a first rate hotel to stay in while they were gone! *[Beat.]* I manage an apartment complex. I've got some wonderful horses. My favorite is Silver. I think he could win the Kentucky Derby. He drinks beer with me.
HERBIE:	This is boring. Let's go. *[Beat.]* Brenda?
BRENDA:	Shut up! I wouldn't have said that ridiculous thing about my horse if you didn't sing about horses drinking beer from that damn country music song.
HERBIE:	You love that song. You're always thinking about it.
BRENDA:	Maybe I need the medicine. *[Beat.]* No one will talk to me except that old lady who I told she had a red and black sock. She said "If you think that's something, I'm wearing a thong too!" *[Beat.]* She went home yesterday. I don't think anything was wrong with her; except being meaner than hell! *[Beat.]* I feel like I'm locked up in prison.
HERBIE:	You are here to stay until they let you out.
BRENDA:	I'm not your good time girl anymore. You get me in trouble—
HERBIE:	Do you want to steal some junk food out of the nurse's station? Potato chips, popsicles, and chocolate. We'll have to eat the popsicles fast.
BRENDA:	All you need is a brain freeze. *[BRENDA and HERBIE cross to the nurse's station.]*
HERBIE:	Stash the loot under your shirt. Nurse is coming. *[BRENDA and HERBIE cross to closet.]* Quick, get in the linen closet. When she leaves we can make a run for it. *[Beat.]* Poke your eye out and see if she's gone.
BRENDA:	I'll have to poke my head out too. *[Covers herself with a sheet and peeks out.]* I look like a ghost. If the other patients see me they'll start screaming.
HERBIE:	*[Giving a James Bond roll]* All hell will break loose! Let's r-o-l-l.
BRENDA:	The popsicles nearly froze my belly off. *[Beat.]* Let's get this

	stuff to the room before we get caught. *[They cross to bedroom.]*
HERBIE:	Go, girl—eat that chocolate. You'll want to p-a-r-t-y!
BRENDA:	I wish I was at home. I would paint my bedroom walls purple with red trim.
HERBIE:	Why don't you wear your leather pants, rockin' t-shirt, spike your hair, and wear your black lipstick? You ain't gonna be able to eat dinner anyway. You'd look hot! *[As HERBIE talks, BRENDA dresses as he suggests.]* Would it help if I sung a little rock'n'roll?
BRENDA:	Give it your best shot.
NURSE BB:	*[Entering BRENDA's room.]* Brenda! What are you doing?
HERBIE:	Tell her you're just fly fishing. [HERBIE mimes fly fishing.]
BRENDA:	I'm dancing.
NURSE BB:	Okay, it's time to eat. Did you dress for dinner?
BRENDA:	It's my favorite look. I can't believe it's time for dinner. Like it?
NURSE BB:	It's different.
HERBIE:	*[Crossing with BRENDA to dinner table area.]* How are you going to eat those noodles with brown stuff after you ate all that junk?
BRENDA:	This is gagging me. I think I'm going to puke.
HERBIE:	Stop that! The guard will call the nurse for sure.
BRENDA:	*[Mimes pouring milk.]* I'm not eating this slop!
HERBIE:	Geez, Brenda why did you pour milk over the noodles? *[Beat.]* You know the rules. You'll be locked up for twenty-four hours. You don't even get to go piss by yourself.
NURSE BB:	*[Crossing to BRENDA.]* I think we need to take you to your room. How much chocolate did you eat?
BRENDA:	I only had one candy bar.
NURSE BB:	Brenda, we found all the wrappers. You're more manic now and need more medicine. *[NURSE BB hands BRENDA pills. Scene moves to BRENDA's room.]*
HERBIE:	You're good! You slipped those pills between your fingers.
BRENDA:	You have to be good to survive in this place.
HERBIE:	You haven't told them about me, have you? They'll put you in a padded cell if you do.
BRENDA:	Don't worry, I wouldn't tell anyone about an ass like you. *[Beat.]* Let's search everybody's rooms. I'll see if they've got any loot I want. I could use some new pajamas. If the nurse sees me I'll tell her I've been doing laundry and using the suitcase for carrying it. *[BRENDA and HERBIE exit carrying suitcase and return moments later.]*
NURSE BB:	Brenda, would you please come into your room?
HERBIE:	I think you've been caught.
BRENDA:	I suppose you're an innocent bystander.

NURSE BB:	Brenda, there are some things missing from everyone's rooms. We'll search until we find them. May we look in your room?
BRENDA:	It wouldn't do me much good to say no would it?
NURSE BB:	Brenda, I'll have to take the suitcase to the lounge and let everyone pick out their things. *[Exits with case.]*
HERBIE:	It was nice of that old biddy to not make you go face the music in front of everyone.
BRENDA:	I don't know why I wanted their old stuff anyway. *[Beat.]* I think I'm just going crazy with nothing to do. *[Beat.]* The lounge is filthy. *[NURSE BB enters bedroom area.]* Nurse, they're pigs around here. The lounge needs cleaning. Can I clean it?
NURSE BB:	Sure. I'll be back in a bit to give you more medicine. *[Exits.]*
HERBIE:	*[During HERBIE's speech, BRENDA cleans.]* Girl, you're in bad shape. I hate it when you get in these stupid cleaning moods. You always act like you're trying to kill whatever you're cleaning, and it makes me tired!
NURSE BB:	*[Enters.]* What have you done? You've moved all that heavy furniture and even mopped the floor! I can't take my eyes off you for a minute! *[Beat.]* I think we had better get this medicine in you now!
HERBIE:	I warned you about the crazy cleaning you do. You'll have to pretend to take it again. *[NURSE BB exits.]*
BRENDA:	The nurse is beautiful isn't she?
HERBIE:	But she knows it. She acts like a snob, with her nose stuck up in the air.
BRENDA:	I asked for something to help me sleep at two o'clock, and she still hasn't given me anything. *[Beat.]* She told me to lie down for twenty minutes. *[Beat.]* I threw my medicine stash in the commode. If she doesn't give me something soon, I'll be ready to jump out the window, and it has bars!
HERBIE:	Why didn't you save some of your medicine in case of an emergency? Hell, you might want to take a permanent sleep in this place, and you wouldn't have any pills to do it with.
BRENDA:	You know they search the room every day for drugs.
HERBIE:	They take away your bra, shoe strings, and belt so you can't hang yourself either. I think it is pretty shitty to make you run around with your teats and shoes flopping! *[Beat.]* They would be in a hell of a lot of trouble if you could stash your pills. You would pass them around just to see the effect on those unfriendly bastards in the lounge.
BRENDA:	I wish you would be quiet for a while and get off my bed. How can I rest with your big ass in the way? *[Beat.]* Here she comes. *[NURSE BB enters and gives BRENDA pills. BRENDA*

slips them in her ear.]

HERBIE:	Atta girl! How did you manage that, pretend to rub your ear and stick your Xanax in it?
NURSE BB:	Do you have an earache?
BRENDA:	It's just itching.
HERBIE:	You know, you could probably be a pickpocket! *[NURSE BB exits.]*
BRENDA:	Sounds like fun, but I'd hate to be thrown in jail. It's bad enough to be locked in here. *[Beat.]* I don't want to think about that or my claustrophobia will kick in, and I'll have a panic attack, and I'll have to stay here longer.
HERBIE:	For God's sake, don't be having a panic attack! You know it takes my breath away. *[Beat.]* You wouldn't want me to have a heart attack would you?
BRENDA:	W-e-l-l, I don't want to hurt your feelings, but sometimes you talk too much. I would like to get rid of you.
HERBIE:	You sure do know how to hurt a guy's feelings. Just for that I'm going to leave you! *[HERBIE exits.]*
BRENDA:	Mom and Dad will be back from the Bahamas sometime this week. *[Beat.]* They just didn't want to fool with me. I hope they burned their asses off. *[BRENDA lies down, tosses and turns.]*
NURSE BB:	*[Enters.]* Why can't you sleep in this comfortable room?
BRENDA:	You know I'm crazy.
NURSE BB:	You said it.
BRENDA:	You are one beautiful bitch!
NURSE BB:	*[Exits, talking to herself.]* Her meds don't seem to be working today.
BRENDA:	Herbie, where are you? I need you. I'm going crazy in here all by myself. *[Beat.]* I called myself crazy again, and you know you don't like that word! I need to tell you something.
HERBIE:	*[Enters.]* I knew you couldn't get along without me.
BRENDA:	Nurse BB made me madder than hell.
HERBIE:	Who in the world is Nurse BB, and what did she do to you?
BRENDA:	BB means Beautiful Bitch. *[Beat.]* You know how we decided we could call me crazy, but no one else could damn well do it? Well, Nurse BB found a way.
HERBIE:	I know how to fix her, but we'll have to sneak into the linen closet and watch for her to leave the nurse's station. *[Beat.]* Have you still got the Xanax?
BRENDA:	If it hasn't melted in my ear.
HERBIE:	We need it. When BB leaves the nurse's station, we'll slip your Xanax into that bottle of water she drinks all the time. She'll fall asleep and get in t-r-o-u-b-l-e!
BRENDA:	*[Removing pill from ear.]* I hope the Xanax has ear wax on it.

HERBIE:	Hurry, there she goes. Get the Xanax into the water.
BRENDA:	*[Crosses to the nurse's station and drops pill into water bottle.]* The water is laced, just waiting for her to drink it. *[NURSE BB enters, drinks.]*
HERBIE:	We should stay in the linen closet until she falls asleep.
BRENDA:	We're going to be cramped in here. *[NURSE BB falls asleep. Lights change to indicate time passing.]* Nurse BB's supervisor really let the sleeping beauty have it!
HERBIE:	We got rid of BB!
BRENDA:	It's her fault for not making sure I took the pill. *[NURSE BB enters.]*
HERBIE:	She's back! Say you don't need the medicine. She might try to poison you.
BRENDA:	I'm taking it! You just talk, talk, talk! *[Takes the medicine. NURSE BB exits.]*
HERBIE:	I might quit talking to you. How would you like that?
BRENDA:	I haven't slept in the last three days. My mind and body are going faster than the Indy 500. I'm getting ready to crash. Go away. I'm going to bed.
HERBIE:	Well! Don't count on me being around when you need me again. *[BRENDA covers her head and snores.]* I've gotten attached to the poor thing. She'll call me back. *[Struts off stage.]*
	[Blackout.]
	[End.]

Author Note *from playwright* Gail Livesay

I have bipolar disorder. *Ward 101* was written from my own experiences and the experiences of others I met while being hospitalized.
I wrote the play as a comedy. Some of it is true and some is fiction.
I guess I wanted to make a statement about mental illness.
I put one or two serious lines in the play—just enough to show that mental patients do not choose the different moods they have.

A Home Like No Place

Carolyn Bertram-Arnold

Characters:
MAXINE   Mid-40s, home only because her mother is ill
TRUDY   Late 30s, dutiful daughter who stayed around,
                MAXINE's younger sister
NURSE   Any age

Time: Early December 2001
Place: A small town called No Place
Setting: A surgical waiting room

[At rise, TRUDY paces back and forth, glancing at her watch every few seconds. MAXINE enters with an overnight bag in each hand, wearing a backpack. When she sees TRUDY, she drops her bags and reaches out her arms. TRUDY pulls away.]

MAXINE: Trudy! Is that you?
TRUDY: Maxine? What are you doing here?
MAXINE: What? No hug for your big sister?
TRUDY: I don't even know you. Your head was shaved last time. Maxi, how—
MAXINE: Actually, it's Sunshine now. I changed it legally.
TRUDY: How did you even find Mama?
MAXINE: She sent me a postcard. Can you believe it? Only a postcard,

	after she kicked me out years—
TRUDY:	She DID NOT kick you out! You left! Do you know how much I hated you for that?
MAXINE:	Oh, Trudy. How could you think that? You'll never know how many times I wanted to come home. I begged—
TRUDY:	You ran away. I remember. I'd just turned 12—the worst year of my life. We were both devastated. You were my idol, you know.
MAXINE:	Me, the wayward daughter, the black sheep of the family, being an idol? Hey! I've not seen you in over twenty-five years, and this is my welcome. What's wrong with us? We're supposed to be here for Mama. Have you heard anything yet?
TRUDY:	*[Glancing at her watch.]* They should tell us something any time. I hope they hurry. I've got to do inventory.
MAXINE:	Mama could be dying, and you're going back to work.
TRUDY :	Mama's healthy as a horse. Her doctor said so or he wouldn't let her…
MAXINE:	Her postcard sounded so urgent. What's going on here?
TRUDY:	What did she tell you?
MAXINE:	*[Pulling postcard from her purse.]* It says, and I quote: "Having part of stomach removed. Would love to see you before I die. Mom." *[Handing postcard to TRUDY.]* Does she have cancer?
TRUDY:	Oh, Mama. She has such a flair for the dramatic. That part in summer theater has done gone to her head. That was her way of getting you to come back home for sure. *[Sarcastically.]* And here you are! My dearest sister, Mama is having a tummy tuck.
MAXINE:	At her age? I can't believe it!
TRUDY:	I tried to talk some sense into her. I thought surely the doctor would discourage…
MAXINE:	A tummy tuck?
TRUDY:	I don't know if I trust him, although he's done thousands— he has women waiting in line.
MAXINE:	What in the world possessed her? I know it's the rage in California, but here in No Place? I'm shocked! Since when is she so concerned about her appearance?
TRUDY:	Since she started going to the Senior Citizens Center twice a week, and square dancing.
MAXINE:	Mama square dancing? Are you sure we have the same Mama? My Mama was the strictest, most religious woman I've ever known. I wasn't allowed to go to my senior prom because there was dancing. *[Laughing.]* Of course, I had my ways of sneaking out.
TRUDY:	Yeah, me, too. Easy, since Mama always went to bed with the chickens.

MAXINE:	And you know what we always said about that?
TRUDY and MAXINE:	*[In unison, giggling.]* Go to bed with the chickens, wake up with feathers in your butt.
TRUDY:	*[Hugging MAXINE.]* Oh, Maxi. I've missed you so much.
MAXINE:	I missed you terribly. But I sure don't miss that name. Can you please call me Sunshine?
TRUDY:	It'll be hard. *[Beat.]* It fits, though. Mama always said she'd rather see you than to see the sunshine any day.
MAXINE:	Really? I figured she'd say it was good riddance. All we did was argue. When I told her my plans to travel with Craig cross country for the summer, she said if I left I could never come home again. So I didn't.
TRUDY:	That's what you thought? Oh, Maxi! I mean, Sunshine. Why DO you hate your name so bad? It can't be any worse than Gertrude.
MAXINE:	Oh, yeah? Well, at least we called you Trudy. Maxi wasn't so bad until high school. But you know how adolescent boys are—such jerks! Every time I'd walk down the hall one of the idiots would yell, "Hey, anybody on the rag? Need a Maxi Pad? Here's one." And they'd point at me.
TRUDY:	Yeah, stupid jerks!
MAXINE:	I gave Clarence a bloody nose once. *[Laughing.]* Know what I did after I punched him?
TRUDY:	What?
MAXINE:	I politely reached in my purse and threw a real Maxi pad at him. I said, "Looks like you're the one needs a Maxi pad now."
TRUDY:	*[Glancing at watch.]* Where all did you and Craig go? Did you see all fifty states? How—
MAXINE :	Man, baby sister. Which question do you want me to answer first?
TRUDY:	Just tell me everything. I've kept up with you some through your postcards and change-of-address notices. Mama thought she had them hid, but I found them. How many times can one person move? *[Beat.]* I envied your glamorous life.
MAXINE:	*[Removing her shawl and sitting.]* Interesting, maybe, but never glamorous. If you saw some of the dumps I've lived in and some of the men I've—well, never mind.
TRUDY :	*[Wringing her hands.]* You're as bad as Mama for keeping me in suspense.
MAXINE:	I tried to tell Mama I was coming back to start college at Berea in the fall. It was the '70s and I was ready to change the world or at least see it! But you know Mama's argument about living in sin—
TRUDY:	*[Impatiently.]* What happened?

MAXINE:	Well, Mama almost talked me out of it until she said, "If you leave now, don't ever set foot in this house again." I was as stubborn as she was. Look where it got both of us. *[Beat.]* I hopped on that motorcycle and never looked back. At least not for a year or so. I was free—no rules, no one to answer to. And no money. That's where it gets interesting.
TRUDY:	How did you live? Did you…
MAXINE:	I'm getting to that. We slept in a tent in the woods—wherever. We lived in communes a while and got back to nature, big time. We shared everything. I do mean everything! That's the part I couldn't handle. Craig and I were fine alone, but I didn't like sharing him with skanks.
TRUDY:	Ooooooh, gross!
MAXINE:	He was having a high old time, though. When I complained, you can imagine what he told me to do. I was crushed. I'd been a hopeless romantic, but I got cured quick. Next, I traveled around with Dusty in his van until he got bored with me— didn't take long. One day he said, "Peace, Baby," and split. Never saw him again—nor cared to. Made money any way I could after…
TRUDY:	Why couldn't you have just come home? That's all Mama talked about. "When Maxine comes home I'm gonna do this, when Maxine comes home—"
MAXINE:	Too bad she never told me that. I would have swallowed my pride—listen at me, like I had any pride left. I would have hopped on the next bus home. I waited years—then I get a postcard like this. A trick. She never said "I'm sorry" or "I love you" or "kiss"—
TRUDY :	*[Reading the postcard silently.]* She did say she'd love to see you. And you know Mama. That's as close to affection as she's likely to get. Did you forget how it was? I never remember Mama saying "I love you" to either of us. It's not her way.
MAXINE:	Why now? After all these years? Why did she finally contact me?
TRUDY:	I think after September 11, she changed. *[Beat.]* Of course, we all have. But when she got your postcard a few days later, that's all she talked about. "Thank God, Maxi's okay," she'd say.
MAXINE:	Oh, Trudy. I should have tried harder. It's all my fault you were stuck here in No Place with no place to go—waiting on Mama. I'm so sorry you didn't get to have a life.
TRUDY:	Hold on a minute, Maxi–Sunshine! I sure wasn't "waiting on Mama." I can't even keep up with her. Who said I didn't have a life? True, I've not been a world traveler like you. But me and Andy manage a few adventures here and there, if you know

	what I mean.
MAXINE:	Who's Andy?
TRUDY:	You remember A. J. that we growed up with. I call him Andy now.
MAXINE:	Little A. J.? No wonder he doesn't go by his real name. Who wants to be called Andrew Jackson, for Heaven's sake? I was so jealous of him.
TRUDY:	Jealous? Why? Did you have a crush on him?
MAXINE:	Lord, no. He was way too young for me. I was jealous because you spent all your time with him instead of me. You were each other's shadows—always climbing trees, playing cowboys and Indians—it looked like such fun. But I never dreamed you two were romantically inclined. You acted like brother and sister.
TRUDY:	That story helped with Mama, too. Since we were always together, she never suspected a thing when we'd go out to the movies or…
MAXINE:	Let me guess. Mama still thinks you're just friends. *[Sarcastically.]* You'd never live in sin, of course. I suppose you're still sneaking around?
TRUDY:	I work with him every day at Handy Andy's Hardware as secretary and gopher. I see him more than if we were married. He's asked me at least once a month for the past ten years. This way we're still teenagers. *[Giggling.]* But I may have to take him up on his offer soon before he changes his mind. *[Patting her stomach.]* At least it will be born before I'm forty.
MAXINE:	Baby Sister, are you for real? You mean I came home just in time to be an aunt—or an uncle? Ha! How can Mama not know? You still live under the same roof?
TRUDY:	Does anybody ever know anybody else? There's a lot you don't know about me or Mama.
MAXINE:	I was just telling Daddy…
TRUDY:	What? Have you been seeing a psychic?
MAXINE:	I don't need a psychic. Daddy's very much alive and well. He helped me—
TRUDY:	Am I in The Twilight Zone? Mama said he died in a car wreck right after you left. Not long after their divorce. Said he was too messed up for an open casket so she had him cremated. His ashes are in the den on the coffee table.
MAXINE:	That's probably just Mama's cigarette ashes.
TRUDY:	Mama don't smoke! Why would she have lied to me?
MAXINE:	I caught her smoking once—actually, we caught each other smoking.
TRUDY:	Never mind the stupid cigarettes! Maxi, what's going on? How could Mama let me think he was dead? And why didn't he

contact me?

MAXINE: Oh, Trudy! Mama probably felt he was dead to her, so he was dead to everybody. But Daddy tried calling at least once a week the first year or so. Mama always hung up on him He hoped you'd answer just once, but you never did. He sent letters, too. Evidently, Mama burned them.

TRUDY: She'd never let me answer the phone. We did get a lot of wrong numbers. God, it makes sense now! Where is Daddy, then?

MAXINE: In California—just two blocks from me. His latest girlfriend is really nice—

TRUDY: His girlfriend? How could he? Is that why him and Mama split up? Other women?

MAXINE: Hey, calm down. There are two sides to everything. Maybe three or four in this case. I don't know the details. But there was a big ruckus when Mama got kicked out of church.

TRUDY: Yeah, she wouldn't be baptized into that faith. Said she'd been baptized once and refused to do it again for God or anybody.

MAXINE: That's not what Daddy said. He said he caught her with Deacon Aubry red-handed—and red-faced, I might add—in the Sunday School room when they were supposedly cleaning the church. When word got out, they cleaned the church all right. They kicked both of them out.

TRUDY: I can't believe Mama could be such a hypocrite! All this time— oh, my God! It never registered. Dean Aubry? The Dean Aubry that runs that produce stand—now, it makes perfect sense. He drops by—

MAXINE: Mama always did love her, uhm, fruit. *[Winking.]* I guess it makes her human after all.

TRUDY: You're defending her? God, Maxi! I just had a horrible thought. All those times I was sneaking out with Andy, I waited until I heard her snoring. What if it wasn't her snoring?

TRUDY and MAXINE: *[In unison.]* Ewwwwwww! Gross!

MAXINE: Trudy, girl. Can't we just keep all this between us for awhile? We've lost so much time already. I just want to start over. Besides, I think you have a few secrets that's going to be coming out in the open soon. Whatever happened, she's still our Mama. I'm kinda relieved to know she's learned how to live a little. Who knows? Maybe she's more like us than she'd like to admit.

TRUDY: At least I won't feel guilty about leaving her alone when me and Andy tie the knot. Boy, is she gonna be in for a shock. Oh, Maxi—uh, Sunshine! What can happen next?

MAXINE: *[Taking locket from her bag and handing it to TRUDY.]* I was saving this for Christmas, but I want you to have it now. I made it myself. I have my own Internet jewelry company. My business and all my belongings are right there in—

TRUDY : *[Examining the necklace.]* Sunshine! It's gorgeous. That always was my favorite picture of us. Remember when—

NURSE: *[Enters. TRUDY and MAXINE turn toward her.]* Ms. Milburn is in recovery. The surgery went well, but she's still groggy. She keeps asking for somebody named Maxi.

MAXINE: *[Gathering her bags.]* That would be me. I never thought I'd be glad to hear that name again. Thank you.

TRUDY: *[Hugging Maxine.]* Welcome home, big sister! Let the fun begin! *[TRUDY and MAXINE exit, laughing. NURSE follows.]*
[Fade to black.]
[End]

AUTHOR NOTE *from playwright* CAROLYN BERTRAM-ARNOLD

I'm fascinated by unusual Kentucky place names. During tornado warnings, a Lexington weatherman mentioned a place called Nonesuch. That's how I came up with the title. I thought if there can be an actual Nonesuch there can be a No Place. Plus, I liked the play on words.

A Home Like No Place is my first serious attempt at writing a play, except for a couple of productions at a country church years ago, custom made for the small cast. This play was written in 2007 with the Kentucky Women Playwrights Seminar led by Trish Ayers. Most of my stories start with a germ of truth that sparks an idea. But with this play, I can honestly say it is as close to pure fiction as I can make it. Everything I write comes together differently, but once I get the characters named (or they name themselves), it starts to gel. That's what happened in this case. Trudy and Maxine took on a life of their own, and I let them argue/talk/ramble to the point I had to cut more of the play than is left. I say when working on a play, "I don't know why they call it play–it's hard WORK!" Writing is the play part, re-writing/editing/cutting is the work part. It all has it rewards. I'm excited that No Place has found a home!

Homespun

Linda Caldwell

Characters:
ANNE   55, JANE's mother
JANE   30, ANNE's daughter
ELIZA   29, ANNE's grandmother, deceased
MARTHA   49, ELIZA's daughter, deceased

Time: November 2005
Place: Eastern Kentucky
Setting: Home of Anne, and former home to other characters

[At rise, ANNE sits center stage by a steamer trunk, quilt squares stacked on the floor. She separates squares and lays them out. JANE enters from stage right. She wears a light jacket and scarf. She hangs jacket and scarf on coat rack near door.]

JANE: The pretty leaves are all gone, Mom. You never went out to see. *[Beat.]* What you got there?
ANNE: Mama's trunk.
JANE: Where'd you get it?
ANNE: Nellie's room.
JANE: Really, where DID you find it? You know Nellie's room is only a family joke?

ANNE:	*[In a sly tone]* Maybe Nellie is real. I'll never tell.
JANE:	All right, Mom, keep your little secrets. *[Sits down, picks up squares. ANNE smacks JANE'S hand.]*
ANNE:	Stop! You're messing up my quilt.
JANE:	That's an idea. Let's make a quilt.
ELIZA:	*[Enters from stage left, hair pulled back with a ribbon, dressed in a nightgown stained with blood.]* Anne, look at that red piece. 'Twas my dress. Took a spirited woman to wear red.
ANNE:	*[Points to a square.]* That's from great-grandmother Eliza's wedding dress.
JANE:	She got married in red?
ANNE:	She was a scarlet woman.
JANE:	Well, I can guess what that means. *[JANE and ANNE move quilt squares around.]*
ELIZA:	Indeed, I was not! I was married a full year before I came to my confinement with Martha.
MARTHA:	*[Enters from stage left, dressed in calico with apron and bonnet.]* Did someone call my name? What is this place? Looks like home but different. Who are you? Why is everybody dressed so quare? *[Points to ELIZA.]* Your gown's all bloody—
ELIZA:	I'm the mother what died birthing you. *[Beat.]* They are the living. Jane can't see or hear you, but Anne can, so be mindful what you say.
MARTHA:	You're Mama, so who are they? *[Beat.]* Is this our house?
ELIZA:	Why, they are your granddaughter and great-granddaughter. *[Beat.]* And this is our home, but life moves on after you're dead.
MARTHA:	That's Anne? She was just a little tow-head when I died. She got a daughter, too?
ELIZA:	Yes, we all have daughters except our Jane there. She's divorced.
MARTHA:	*[Shocked.]* Divorced!
ANNE:	Don't mention IT. She's not over IT yet.
JANE:	Who ARE you talking to?
ANNE:	Martha and Eliza.
JANE:	Who? What in the hell…
ANNE:	You know they're in the pictures over there.
JANE:	*[Walks to wall stage left, looks at pictures, then turns back, sits.]* Never mind, Mom. You know they really aren't here, don't you?
ANNE:	Not here? Of course they're here.
JANE:	You're in another stage.
ANNE:	Stage of what?
JANE:	Never mind. It's okay, Mom.
ANNE:	Of course it's okay. *[MARTHA looks over ANNE'S and JANE'S shoulders.]*

JANE:	But you know, Mom, we are going to have to start talking about making some changes.
MARTHA:	Those are the last squares I pieced. *[Beat.]* Died out in the garden the day I was going to set them in a quilt. 'Twas this time of year. 'Twas getting in the last of the green tomatoes before frost.
ANNE:	See this square? I helped Granny piece it before she died. *[Beat.]* I won't go into a home.
JANE:	You can move in with me.
ANNE:	*[Sulking.]* This is where my people lived and died. I'll die here, too. *[Cheerful.]* You can move in with me.
JANE:	You can't ask me to do that. I can't.
ELIZA:	There were four generations living here when you were born, Martha.
MARTHA:	People didn't send off their sick and old.
ELIZA:	For the life of me *[Laughs.]* or the death of me, I can't figure out why they put their loved ones away.
MARTHA:	It was a house of grief I grew up in. You died. Grandmama died a little later. Aunt Patsy lived with me and Will until she passed. *[Beat.]* Or maybe you'd say we lived with her. Aunt Patsy sat for hours by the fireplace, quilting day in, day out. Every descendent of Grandmama's got one of Aunt Patsy's quilts.
ANNE:	Jane, remember that picture of Eliza over there? It was taken when she was pregnant with Granny.
JANE:	I can't believe Great-grandmother was a scarlet woman.
ELIZA:	Shame. Came to help you, Anne, and you're telling lies on me.
MARTHA:	Mama, why ARE we here?
ELIZA:	To help Anne's passing.
MARTHA:	Looks the picture of health.
ELIZA:	*[Whispers.]* She's gone. Her body just ain't caught up.
MARTHA:	Always wanted to come back. Can I stay? *[MARTHA touches things, turns lights on and off.]*
ANNE:	Stay. *[Beat.]* Jane'll make tea. *[Beat.]* Sit down, why don't you?
ELIZA:	It won't be like when you was living—
JANE:	Mom. *[Beat.]* You're acting so weird.
ANNE:	Make the tea. Then I'll tell you all about the quilt pieces.
JANE:	I'm afraid to leave the room. *[Aside.]* I don't understand. The doctor's didn't say the changes would happen so fast. She's hallucinating. *[Beat.]* We've got to talk. *[JANE continues to move squares around, and ANNE returns them to original positions.]*
ANNE:	Granny Martha, they go like this, don't they?
ELIZA:	Doctors! They killed me! Said I was too old to have my first

	child. I was only twenty-nine. Too young to die. If they'd let Grace attend to my confinement, I would have lived.
MARTHA:	Grace?
ELIZA:	She was the midwife, but your papa had to get all high-falluting and send for a doctor. Bah!
ANNE:	I can't leave.
ELIZA:	Of course you can't, dear. We're here to help you stay.
MARTHA:	You said—
ELIZA:	Shh. Humor her.
ANNE:	Eliza understands. When you live in a place with all your people before you, you can't leave. *[Beat.]* You've felt the touch of angel-kisses.
JANE:	You are creeping me out.
ANNE:	Always pestering me to hear about your ancestors. I'm trying to collect them for you. They're right here. *[Points to ELIZA and MARTHA and all around the room.]*
JANE:	Let's just go back to the quilt, Mom. *[Moves several squares.]*
ANNE:	Quit. They go like so. *[Beat.]* This was your dress.
JANE:	The fabric is too old—
ANNE:	Damn it. Reckon I know—
MARTHA:	I never heard a woman curse!
ELIZA:	Times change. Sometimes the sickness makes her say worse.
MARTHA:	How do you know?
ELIZA:	Been here for years. Nobody ever saw me before, though.
MARTHA:	*[Shocked.]* Does she have bad blood?
ELIZA:	Just sickness. No such thing as what THEY called bad blood.
ANNE:	Stop talking about unhappy stuff. Jane, I said make the tea. *[Beat.]* You never listen to me anymore.
JANE:	I try, Mom, but you're acting craz—I mean odd. *[Exits.]*
ANNE:	Bring four cups, hear? *[Beat.]* She's such a worry-wart. Wish she'd just leave.
ELIZA:	You told her I was a scarlet woman!
ANNE:	*[Laughs.]* I just wanted to spice things up a bit. She's so righteous about family history.
ELIZA:	She'll be reporting to those prissy ladies in her genealogy club.
MARTHA:	Don't like her thinking I was begat on the wrong side of the blanket.
ANNE:	There's no stigma to illegitimacy now.
MARTHA:	*[Puzzled.]* No stigma? *[Beat.]* Still don't like it.
ELIZA:	Martha, you don't have to worry—
MARTHA:	I'd like to have another chance here.
ELIZA:	You had twenty years on me. *[Exasperated.]* You made quilts from your babies' clothes. *[Beat.]* You made your babies—
MARTHA:	You made me a yellow dress. Aunt Patsy told me.

ELIZA:	*[Strokes MARTHA'S hair.]* Only thing I got to make you. I took to my bed months before you were born, and then I died. *[Beat.]* I knew you was a girl. Did you feel my presence?
MARTHA:	Sometimes I featured you was behind me in the looking glass.
ELIZA:	Now, we got to help Anne pass.
ANNE:	Don't talk about my passing.
ELIZA:	I'm so sorry, dear—
ANNE:	I'm too young.
ELIZA:	You've had longer—
ANNE:	Times're different. There's drugs to cure—
ELIZA:	Medicine can't help what you got.
ANNE:	*[Stands stiffly, walks to table and takes out scissors. Confronts ELIZA.]* I'll just kill myself.
MARTHA:	Surely, she's not supposed to take her own life?
ELIZA:	Be quiet, Martha. *[Beat.]* We at least left with our right minds.
ANNE:	I don't like you talking about me like I'm not here.
MARTHA:	Put the scissors down, dear. Listen to your granny. *[ANNE's hand relaxes around the scissors.]*
JANE:	*[Enters with tea tray, sees scissors.]* Mom, why do you have the scissors? You could hurt—
ANNE:	Stop smothering me!
JANE:	I worry—
ANNE:	Well, don't. I'm fine. Go home.
JANE:	We are going to have our tea and talk about arrange—
ANNE:	Oh. *[Beat.]* Goody. Did you bring cups for Martha and Eliza?
JANE:	*[Wryly.]* Sure, I did. *[Sets tea tray down, pours tea into two cups, mimes pouring tea into two more cups.]*
MARTHA:	*[Picks up her cup.]* I miss tea.
ELIZA:	Yes, you'd think heaven would have tea. *[JANE starts putting sugar in real cups of tea.]*
ANNE:	No tea in heaven? *[Beat.]* Let me sugar my own, please.
JANE:	But I know how you like it.
ANNE:	*[Angrily.]* Don't treat me like an incompetent—
JANE:	Sorry. Just trying to help.
ANNE:	Don't. *[Jerks cup away from JANE. Tea slops on quilt squares.]*
JANE:	Look out!
ANNE:	*[Sing-song]* Never mind. *[Stares blankly.]*
JANE:	It'll stain. *[Beat.]* I'll get some towels. *[Exits. ANNE picks up scissors, cuts quilt squares.]*
MARTHA:	She's ruining the quilt. Stop her!
ELIZA:	We can't interfere now. *[JANE enters with towels.]*
MARTHA:	Why? *[Beat.]* I picked up this cup.
ELIZA:	That only happens in your mind.
MARTHA:	She listened to me before.

ELIZA: She's taken a turn for the worse.
JANE: Mom! What— *[ANNE drops scissors and looks toward MARTHA and ELIZA.]*
MARTHA: What do we do now?
ELIZA: Meet her on the other side.
MARTHA: When?
ELIZA: Soon.
MARTHA: Do you think we helped?
ELIZA: I don't know. This is the first time I ever broke through to anybody. *[Beat.]* Anne, we'll be waiting.
ANNE: *[Picks up scissors.]* Can I come back like you? *[MARTHA and ELIZA exit.]*
ELIZA: *[Answers from offstage.]* If you want to bad enough. *[ANNE exits.]*
JANE: Mom, I'm not ready. Mom, please come back.
                        [Blackout.]
                        [End.]

Author Note *from playwright* Linda Caldwell

Quilt pieces serve as a metaphor for family – transcending illness, death and time.

Painting the Egress

Trish Ayers

Characters:

MAMA   Mid- to late-60s, has Alzheimer's Disease,
              nursing home resident
SISSY   Mid-40s, MAMA's oldest daughter
JANET   Late-30s, MAMA's youngest daughter,
              recently returned from Iraq war

Time: Present
Place: A nursing home
Setting: Mama's private room in the nursing home

[At rise, there is the impression of a hospital bed with an IV pole. During play, MAMA mimes painting on an invisible vertical canvas the shape of a full-size door. MAMA talks to Monet, her deceased dog that neither SISSY nor JANET can see. SISSY and JANET talk to MAMA as if she is in the bed.]

MAMA: *[MAMA slips out of bed, walks to invisible painting.]*
              Swish, dip, drip...Monet, Monet? There you are. Good boy!
              Missed you. Sit. I don't know why they have that crazy...law...I
              mean, rule about no dogs here. I'm glad you figured out how to
              be with me. You're the only one who has.

SISSY:	*[Enters, crosses to bed as if MAMA is in it.]* Afternoon, Mama.
MAMA:	Monet, what color should we paint our exit door?
SISSY:	You look pretty today. Was Becca here? She does a nice job with your hair.
MAMA:	A nice red? I remember my pair of red pumps that Granny gave me. Mama thought they were, well, not something a nice, church-going, southern girl should be seen in...I put them on after I left home and was away from my Mama's vigilant eye!
SISSY:	Did Becca do your nails too?
MAMA:	Doesn't Sissy know she's talking to my empty body? I'm the locust that's been freed from its brittle shell.
SISSY:	This morning I noticed your tulips when I got the mail. They're pretty this year.
MAMA:	Tulips are for still lifes...or to put on graves.
SISSY:	Mama, Bob, your lawyer, says we need to sell the house to help pay for your stay here.
MAMA:	I have no need for that house. Soon I'll be far away from here.
SISSY:	Let me straighten your covers. *[Beat.]* Got an offer today. More than I expected.
MAMA:	Just a bunch of painted wood...and memories.
SISSY:	Janet hasn't answered any of my letters.
MAMA:	She will...in time. Dip...
SISSY:	Wish she'd come back. Wish you would, at least long enough to decide about the house.
JANET:	*[Enters in wheelchair, legs covered.]* Over my dead body! Our homeplace survived the Civil War, thanks to Grandma Wiley.
SISSY:	Janet! I thought you were still in Germany, in the hospital.
JANET:	What gives you the right to sell, to toss our history away like a rotten potato?
SISSY:	They want to transfer Mama to a state nursing home. You know about those places—
JANET:	Sissy, what happened to all of Mama's IRAs and CDs?
SISSY:	Mama's been here for two, no, three years now. It's expensive.
JANET:	I knew I shouldn't have left you in charge of the money—
SISSY:	I did just fine without you.
JANET:	Then how come Mama's broke?
MAMA:	My two sweet babies, spatting at each other again. *[Beat.]* Swish, dip, drip, swish, dip.
SISSY:	I don't want to fight.
JANET:	Fighting's what got me these mangled legs.
MAMA:	Drip...jabber...squabble...jabber.
JANET:	Mama, I missed you so much. *[To SISSY.]* She looks sad.
MAMA:	What color do I need to paint it? Swish...
JANET:	I had the chaplain say a prayer for you every day. He'd come

and sit by my bed, said the most beautiful prayers. It was almost like sitting in the Baptist church right here in town.

MAMA: A nurse that works here talks...prays for you each day. Never was too much on that mumbo jumbo stuff but it did seem to help...swish, drip...like I was closer to you.

SISSY: Mama, it's like old times with Janet back. Remember how we'd pack a picnic lunch and walk in the woods?

JANET: And play in the wild flowers I was allergic to.

SISSY: Shhh! Mama might hear you.

JANET: That's about as likely as you listening to me.

SISSY: Janet!

MAMA: Swish...drip...Monet, let me see if I can find your bone. It's here somewhere...I know I put it...here it is. I know how you love them.

JANET: *[Holds up an open bag of bones.]* Is this where all Mama's money's gone?

SISSY: The bones comfort Mama. She clings to them at night. She talks about Monet—

JANET: Monet's been dead for years. *[Beat.]* How can she remember him and not us?

SISSY: I don't think Mama's ever gotten over losing him.

JANET: I think Mama has never forgiven me...I didn't see Monet until too late. I can still hear his yelp when I backed down the driveway. I slammed the car in park and jumped out. There was Monet, covered in blood, his eyes looked up at me so trusting, almost begging me to fix him as he convulsed. I held him in my arms until he stopped breathing. *[Beat.]* There's a bone missing. Where is it?

SISSY: In a drawer?

JANET: Bet that nurse gets us to buy bones for her house full of dogs! You gotta watch everything in these places. You don't leave money lying around in Mama's room?

MAMA: Monet, remind me to hide your...what are they? Bones... bones aren't as easy to set free, they don't evaporate like the words in my brain.

SISSY: It's hard to look at Mama. She's in a different world.

JANET: How long has she been like this?

SISSY: A bit of her would disappear each day until she didn't even open her eyes when I came.

JANET; Why bother coming?

SISSY: False hope. I struggle with denial. Every time I open this door I hope, dream, that a miracle happened and I would get to see her eyes twinkle and her smile...

JANET: Come on, sis, you of all people should know better.

MAMA:	Silly girl, wastes her...minutes here when life is outside these doors. Drip...
JANET:	Doc Brown warned us.
SISSY:	Did he tell us I'd lose my life to Mama's disease?
JANET:	Come on, Sis, you don't need to be so dramatic.
MAMA:	Swish...I dream, want to finish this painting so I can paint with my artist friends.
SISSY:	I had to give up my practice.
JANET:	Here we go again. Do you have to rub your clinical psychologist doctorate in my face?
SISSY:	You have to understand.
JANET:	I don't.
SISSY:	Three years of this, my mind feels like it's gone. I barely speak in complete sentences.
JANET:	Come on. My intellectual sis?
SISSY:	It's been years since I've been to the movies. I tried to hire someone to take care of Mama. No one wanted the job. My friends disappeared—
MAMA:	They weren't your friends, dear daughter. Dip...
JANET:	Sis, Mama's right here! It's terrible to have people talk about you when you're right smack in front of them. Trust me. I know.
SISSY:	Oh, Mama, I didn't mean...remember all of your friends spending weekends painting, arguing, and drinking? I wish I'd kept some of the sketches they did for me.
JANET:	They'd be worth a fortune. There aren't any in the studio? There were stacks of—
SISSY:	She always had a canvas ready for us. [Beat.] Mama's the reason I went to Paris to study.
MAMA:	Paris, artists, the smell of oils filled the air. [Beat.] I need to get back to work. Dip...
JANET:	I thought you wanted to see what was beyond these hills and Mama's nagging. That's why I joined the Marines. I couldn't stand Mama looking at me like I was a failure.
SISSY:	Wanted to meet Mama's friends. The ones she talked about painting with, before us.
JANET:	Did you figure out which one was our Daddy?
SISSY:	Janet!
JANET:	Well, did you?
SISSY:	Another secret that'll die with Mama.
JANET:	My Dad probably wasn't an artist. I never fit in—
MAMA:	Splatter, drip, dip. [Beat.] Janet was an odd girl. She could sit for hours and play with, what are they called? Not letters, numbers. I had to tug at her to even try to paint, draw—

SISSY:	Mama, look at you, you're all scrunched up. Is that better? *[Mimes moving MAMA into a better position.]*
JANET:	Sis, you know she won't answer?
SISSY:	I miss the sound of her voice.
JANET:	Which one? Her voice changed. Two years ago I tried to call her from Iraq and kept hanging up because I thought I got the wrong number. *[Beat.]* There's a—was a vulnerability, like she lacked confidence in getting the next word out.
SISSY:	She sounded like a child.
JANET:	You did notice!
SISSY:	Not until you mentioned it. You know how it is when you're around someone daily—
JANET:	Is that another jab at me for not being around?
SISSY:	Why do you always play the victim?
JANET:	Sis, try looking at my legs. Oh, that's right, you won't look at them. No one does. So I hide these under this quilt, the one Mama made for me.
SISSY:	I'm not talking about your...your...injury.
MAMA:	I made Janet her quilt to keep her warm at night. Sissy had her work. Swish, dip, swish.
JANET:	Have you ever asked me what happened? How it felt to have my legs blown out from under me? You know how I was known for my long and lean legs. I didn't want to live—
SISSY:	Mama kept escaping from the house, even with the alarm system. One day I found her in the middle of the road, stark naked, with her easel, painting.
JANET:	It was pretty damn lousy lying in that stinking hospital bed. No one to talk to. The guys weren't interested in me anymore. They spent their time flirting with the women nurses and doctors, not a broken down woman soldier with mangled legs.
SISSY:	You could have written. Mama used to stumble up the gravel road every day, convinced there'd be a letter from you. I always followed, trying to hide behind the pines—
JANET:	The only letters I got from you described the "deterioration" of Mama in your usual "sterile clinical" mumbo jumbo. I didn't care what stage Mama was in.
SISSY:	I thought you should...would want to kno—
JANET:	They ripped the burned skin off my legs, hours of torture, worse than the explosion. I wanted you to come see me.
SISSY:	I couldn't leave Mama—
JANET:	I couldn't help with Mama! *[Angrily exits.]*
MAMA:	*[Paints.]* Dip, drip. Monet, those two will work things out. We'll be leaving this all behind—
SISSY:	Mama, Janet—she's different since her injury.

MAMA:	Hospitals change you.
SISSY:	She isn't ready to sell the house but we have to do something.
MAMA:	Give her time. This world can be overwhelming. A little white here, for highlights.
SISSY:	My friend Beatrice's mom was in a state home. Beatrice found her mom covered in bedsores, hadn't been turned for days, filthy, left to rot in her own body fluids.
MAMA:	Splatter...drip...let things go. Let me go. [JANET enters.]
SISSY:	You're back?
JANET:	Where'd you expect me to go?
SISSY:	I thought you'd left me alone again...to make all the decisions—
JANET:	Look, I talked to that administrator—
SISSY:	I don't want to hear what that idiot has to say. I need something to eat. [Exits.]
JANET:	[Rolls up next to bed.] Mama, I knew it wasn't your fault you couldn't come. [Beat.] Can you hear me?
MAMA:	I was with you in that place where they help you—hospital. I left my shell to be with you—
JANET:	I wrote a check to cover six months here. Couldn't stand for you to go to a state home.
MAMA:	Don't waste your money. Monet and I have other plans.
JANET:	Sis doesn't need to know the money came from me. I could have been more help, at least written her. I wanted to run as far away as I could. I couldn't stand the thought of you disappearing right before my eyes. I thought it would be easier if I ignored it.
MAMA:	How about some highlights right here, Monet?
JANET:	Mama, I may sound crazy, but I felt you with me...when I was lying on the ground in that pool of blood. I swear I felt your hand on my shoulder and your breath on my face.
MAMA:	I rubbed your shoulder as you convulsed in pain...rub, soothe, rub, love, dip, brush—
JANET:	I don't know if Sis told you—I almost didn't make it. Sometimes I wish I hadn't. [Beat.] I brought something to show you. I'll never be the artist you dreamed...I took up drawing when I was trapped in bed. I got pretty good. See? [Pulls out sketch pad, shows it over bed. MAMA crosses to see.]
SISSY:	[Enters, sees the drawings. JANET puts pad away, and SISSY hands her a burger.] Burger or cheeseburger?
JANET:	Burger! Oh man, a good old fashioned American hamburger, dripping with ketchup and mustard.
SISSY:	I had them add extra cheese. You're looking a bit scrawny.
JANET:	Still my older sis, huh?

SISSY:	I've missed you.
JANET:	There were so many nights I wanted to call you up but I figured you had your hands full with Mama and all.
SISSY:	You should have called. I worried about you too. What are we going to do about Mama?
JANET:	No need to bother your head about that now.
SISSY:	But—
JANET:	When I rolled out of here huffing and puffing mad at you. I high tailed it to the administrator's office. It seems the nursing home bookkeeper made a stupid mistake. Mama can stay here at least six more months. Our home place is safe. *[Beat.]* Truce?
SISSY:	Oh, Janet! Bless your heart.
JANET:	Remember the times we sat on the front porch? Mama in the chair and us in the swing.
SISSY:	Mama made the best sweet tea. Never got her recipe. It's lost now. There's been too much loss—
JANET:	I'm back, I'll help. It's time I do my part—
MAMA:	*[Finishes painting with a flourish.]* Swish...lilt...swish...finally! My work is done! Leonardo, here we come.
SISSY:	I don't think Mama would mind being by herself a few minutes. We could go outside and eat at the picnic table... would you bring your drawings? Please? *[Beat.]* Mama, we'll be back in a few minutes. *[Beat.]* I love you.
JANET:	We love you. *[They exit.]*
MAMA:	Come on, Monet, your namesake is waiting for us. *[Mimes opening the completed painting of the imaginary door and exits.]*

[Blackout.]

[Sound of door closing and a dog's bark.]

[End.]

AUTHOR NOTE *from playwright* TRISH AYERS

The day I was told my mother had been diagnosed with Alzheimer's,
I pondered what it would mean.
The thought of this vibrant woman slipping away and
unable to communicate while trapped in her body terrified me.

I had to find a way to accept this,
so I turned to playwriting and asked the question,
"What is it like for the person in the final stages of Alzheimer's?"
Then the character of Mama walked into my writing life.
She began to speak in sound bites that mimicked the beats
of the medical equipment she was surrounded by,
and to my surprise she arose out of bed
and began to chat with a dog from her past
while she painted on a canvas that was only in her head.

As her daughters entered the play, it was clear there were
some issues dividing the once close sisters.
Sissy, who had cared for Mama over the years, made the decision
to give up her job, friends and life so she could be with Mama.
Janet had escaped her hometown by means of joining the service
and paid the price with mangled legs from a bomb explosion.
Each sister felt deserted.
So, I let the sisters free to do as they wanted,
all the while Mama continued to paint the door for her final exit.

After I completed this play, my mother called me
excited that now that she had hearing aids
she could hear what everyone was saying.
Soon, it became clear that most of my mother's symptoms
of being disconnected were related to her hearing
and that she did not have Alzheimer's.
Now that's what I call a happy ending!

Remembering Rosemary
A short play in five scenes

ANNE SHELBY

Characters:

NELL	70s. She is carrying a purse.
BOBBIE	Early 50s, NELL's daughter. She carries a disorganized stack of books, maps, brochures and papers about Maysville and about Rosemary Clooney.
VIVIAN	Late 40s, BOBBIE's sister. She is carrying a camera.
ASHLEY	19, VIVIAN's daughter. She is wearing a University of Kentucky sweatshirt.

Time:	The present
Place:	Maysville, Kentucky
Setting:	Outdoors

Scene 1. *The River*

VIVIAN: *[With camera.]* Scrooch in a little closer to Mama, Bobbie. You, too, Ashley, honey. That's good. Big smiles, girls. *[Snaps photo.]* Okay, got it. I wanted one of you all with the river in the background.

ASHLEY: Wow, it's big.

NELL: Well, of course it's big, honey. It's the Ohio River. It's supposed

	to be big.
VIVIAN:	I wonder if Rosemary Clooney ever stood right where I'm standing and looked at the river going by.
BOBBIE:	Could be. I read somewhere that she used to sit on her grandmother's porch as a kid, watching the Ohio.
NELL:	What was she thinking, I wonder.
BOBBIE:	She said she thought there might be good times waiting, somewhere down the river.
ASHLEY:	What's that?
NELL:	That's the floodwall. You've seen a floodwall before, haven't you, at Barbourville and Pineville?
ASHLEY:	Not like that.
NELL:	Yes, I do believe Maysville has the nicest floodwall.
VIVIAN:	I like those big pictures painted on it.
BOBBIE:	Oh, look, there's two of Rosemary!
ASHLEY:	Murals, Mother. They're called murals.
VIVIAN:	*[In a mocking tone.]* Murals. They're called murals. Well, they look like pictures to me.
BOBBIE:	According to the unofficial Rosemary Clooney website, if we walk from here up to East Second Street, we should come to Rosemary's grandmother's house.
NELL:	Well, if I'd known I was going to have to walk all over Maysville, I'd have worn comfortable shoes.
ASHLEY:	I'd have brought a jacket.
VIVIAN:	I'd have worn a better bra.
BOBBIE:	Okay, we've come all the way up here from Corbin. Let's try not to whine the whole time.
ASHLEY:	Well, you all dragged me up here. So what's the big deal about Rosemary Clooney?
NELL:	Well, she was a big star!
BOBBIE:	And one great singer.
VIVIAN:	She did records, concerts. She made movies. And didn't she have her own TV show, Mama? In the '50s? I can almost remember it.
NELL:	She most certainly did. She had two shows, "The Rosemary Clooney Show" and—
BOBBIE:	*[Imitating announcer.]* "The Lux Show Starring Rosemary Clooney!"
NELL:	And every time she'd come on the television, Harold would say—
BOBBIE and VIVIAN:	*[In unison.]* "She's from Kentucky!"
VIVIAN:	It was like he was proud of her or something.
NELL:	Well, he was! We all were. She was from Kentucky!
ASHLEY:	Talk about a cultural inferiority complex.

BOBBIE: Maybe it was all those brier jokes he had to listen to at the Ford plant in Cincinnati.

VIVIAN: "Why did they build a bridge over the Ohio River?"

VIVIAN and BOBBIE: "So the Kentuckians could swim over in the shade." *[Dryly.]* Yuk yuk yuk.

ASHLEY: People still tell jokes like that. I hear 'em all the time. Especially on TV. Like we're all stupid, racist, incestuous—

NELL: So when somebody like Rosemary Clooney comes along.... And she was not just a big star, she was—

BOBBIE and VIVIAN: —a nice person.

BOBBIE: And that voice. You cannot describe it, but there's something about it that is so right. You know it when you hear it. You know it's Rosemary.

VIVIAN: "The best friend a song ever had," they call her.

BOBBIE: That might be it there, the white brick.

VIVIAN: That's it?

NELL: Yes, Vivian. What did you expect?

VIVIAN: I don't know. It just looks so—I don't know—ordinary.

NELL: I think it's nice. Rosemary was a girl in that house.

VIVIAN: Is this her Grandmother Clooney's house?

BOBBIE: The other one, I think. Grandmother Guilfoyle.

ASHLEY: How come she lived with her grandmother?

BOBBIE: Her parents were separated. I think her dad drank. Anyway, he was gone a lot, and her mother was gone a lot, too, so the kids—

NELL: —Rosemary and Betty and Nick—

BOBBIE: —stayed with first one and then another, whoever would take them, usually their grandparents.

VIVIAN: That is so sad.

ASHLEY: How come you all know so much about Rosemary Clooney?

BOBBIE: Liner notes. Websites.

VIVIAN: Entertainment network, honey.

BOBBIE: And she wrote two autobiographies.

NELL: I just always followed Rosemary. One time when Vivian was a baby, and Rosemary had become popular, it was my birthday. And I saw in the newspaper one of those "Famous People Born on This Day" articles, and it said "Rosemary Clooney." We were born the same day, Rosemary and me, May 23. I liked her before that, but I just paid more attention to her then. Of course, she didn't know me from Adam's housecat. But I just always did love Rosemary Clooney. I felt like we were related some way.

Scene 2. The Russell

BOBBIE: Look! It's the Russell! The old Russell Theatre! Rosemary sang there when she was just a little girl. She said there were stars on the ceiling.

VIVIAN: Looks like they're restored it.

NELL: The Russell Theatre. Now you all will not remember this—but it was a very big deal at the time. They had the world premiere of Rosemary's first movie right here at the Russell Theatre in Maysville, Kentucky. And thousands of people came and filled up the town. There was a parade, and Rosemary had on her new mink coat, and with that blonde pageboy—well, it was just like Cinderella. They named a street after her. And I believe she auctioned off fifteen-hundred pounds of burley tobacco as part of the festivities.

BOBBIE: She sang at the premiere that night, on the same stage where she sang as a little girl, in the old Russell Theatre, with the stars on the ceiling.

ASHLEY: What was the name of the movie?

BOBBIE: "The Stars Are Singing."

ASHLEY: Never heard of it.

NELL: Well, did you ever hear of "White Christmas," Miss Smarty Britches?

ASHLEY: That was her?

NELL: That came out in 1954. I remember because Harold took me to Lexington to see it in the '54 Chevy and it was brand new.

ASHLEY: Did you and Papaw go to Lexington to see movies sometimes?

NELL: No, we never went to Lexington to see movies. That was what was so special about it. We drove up old highway 25 to Lexington and spent the night at the Phoenix Hotel and saw Rosemary Clooney in "White Christmas." And, oh, she was wonderful. She sang like a bird—and those dresses! Nobody looked better in a dress then than Rosemary.

VIVIAN: Is that the one where they sing about snow?

BOBBIE, VIVIAN and NELL: *[Singing.]* Snow snow snow snow snow!

BOBBIE: It's also the one where they sing "Sisters," remember?

VIVIAN: I had completely forgotten that! We used to sing that! We'd break off little tree branches and wave them around like Rosemary and Vera Ellen's fans.

BOBBIE and VIVIAN: *[Singing.]* Sisters, sisters — There were never such devoted sisters . . .

BOBBIE: Big finish—

BOBBIE and VIVIAN: *[Singing.]* Lord help the mister who comes between me and my sister, and Lord help the sister who comes between me and my man.

Scene 3. St. Patrick's Church

BOBBIE:	I think if we walk on down the street in this direction, we should come to St. Patrick's.
ASHLEY:	Did she have any hit songs?
NELL:	*[Singing.]* Come on a my house, my house a come on
VIVIAN and BOBBIE:	*[Singing.]* I'm gonna give you apple, plum and apricot, too
NELL:	*[Singing.]* Peach and pear and mango, too
ASHLEY:	Oh. My. God. You all have to promise me you will never do that again.
VIVIAN:	I think we sound pretty good.
BOBBIE:	We do sound good.
NELL:	We sound right nice, if I do say—
ASHLEY:	Well, it's not the singing so much as the latent sexual content of the lyrics. And sung by my mother, my grandmother and my aunt—you're freaking me out, okay?
NELL:	What in God's name is the child talking about?
VIVIAN:	I don't know, Mother. I've not understood a word she said since she started to college. What is "latent sexual content"?
ASHLEY:	Latent sexual content is latent sexual content!
NELL:	Vivian, can't you make her stop saying that?
ASHLEY:	It's a song about sex, Mother. It's just disguised because the 1950s were such a repressive era in American cultural history.
NELL:	Ashley Heather Renee Maggard! I hope you are not turning into one of those people who think everything is about sex. "Come On-A My House" may be silly, but it is a nice song sung by a nice girl who is inviting a friend to her home to enjoy some fresh fruit.
BOBBIE and VIVIAN:	*[Cackling, ad libbing.]* Yeah, right, fruit salad, okay.
NELL:	Girls, we are at the church house!
BOBBIE:	St. Patrick's.
NELL:	This is where Rosemary went to church and was baptized and took her first communion. I bet she went to Catholic school right next door there.
VIVIAN:	And this is where she and Dante got married.
NELL:	It's where they had her funeral. I saw it in the Lexington paper. There was a big crowd.
ASHLEY:	Okay. I'll bite. Who's Dante?
VIVIAN:	What do they teach you in college? Dante is Rosemary's second husband.
NELL:	Her first was that Jose Ferrer. He had a wandering eye.
VIVIAN:	It wasn't just his eye that wandered, Mama.
NELL:	I know that, Vivian. We are on a public street. I was trying to be—

BOBBIE: In her autobiography? This is awful. They're on their honey-moon in Europe and she finds out he has already been unfaithful to her.

VIVIAN: Between the wedding and the honeymoon he did it? Lord, that's worse than Larry.

ASHLEY: That's it. I am never getting married in my life. If I ever even start to get married, I want you to shoot me. Really, you have my permission.

VIVIAN: All right, dear.

NELL: Whatever you want, sweetheart.

BOBBIE: We promise.

NELL: But Rosemary just should never have married that Jose Ferrer. I said it at the time, I still say it today, and I don't care who knows it. She could have married that nice Dante in the first place, and saved herself a lot of trouble. But she ran off and married Jose Ferrer and had a big gang of children by him just as quick as she could have them, and him playing around the whole time. It makes me so mad—

VIVIAN: But I think she loved him, Mama, and he loved her. They just couldn't get along. Just because you're in love with somebody, doesn't mean you can get along with them.

ASHLEY: Oh no. Then it's worse than I thought. Everything is worse than I thought.

NELL: Of course it is, dear. You're nineteen. But Rosemary did end up with Dante, a very nice man, so it was a happy ending.

ASHLEY: Yeah, but the whole middle part sucked.

VIVIAN: Ashley!

ASHLEY: Well, it did!

Scene 4. Street near Grandmother Guilfloyle's house

BOBBIE: Okay, West Third. We should be about to Grandmother Guilfoyle's house, which is on the National Register of Historic Places.

ASHLEY: I thought we already saw Grandmother Guilfoyle's house.

BOBBIE: It's a different house.

NELL: People move, honey. They move, they gain weight—

VIVIAN: They eat fruit.

BOBBIE: I wonder if that's it.

ASHLEY: Yeah, there's a sign. "National Register of Historic Places. Home of singer Rosemary Clooney."

NELL: Look, you can see the river from this house, too.

BOBBIE: And look! Look at the sign on the corner!

ASHLEY: *[Reading.]* "Rosemary Clooney Street." She did have a street named after her.

NELL:	Yes, and she deserved it, too. She was a big star and—
ALL:	—a nice person.
VIVIAN:	Yes, Mama, we all love Rosemary, but aren't you leaving something out? You always do that. You just remember the parts you want to remember. Everything else, you just pretend like it didn't happen.
NELL:	*[Covering her ears.]* I do not want to listen to this today, Vivian!
VIVIAN:	*[Pulling NELL's hands away from her ears.]* Mama, everybody knows Rosemary Clooney got hooked on pills and went nuts.
NELL:	Vivian!
VIVIAN:	She did, Mama! I saw it on "E! True Hollywood Story!"
ASHLEY:	Mom watches "E!" like other people read the Bible.
VIVIAN:	I read the Bible!
BOBBIE:	Rosemary talked about her nervous breakdown quite openly. She'd gotten addicted to sleeping pills—
VIVIVAN:	Like Elvis—
NELL:	—and Judy Garland—
BOBBIE:	Yeah, and a bunch of other people. Apparently they used to hand pills out to performers like mints. And she became psychotic. She was in therapy for a long time.
NELL:	Well, that Jose Ferrer would drive anybody—
BOBBIE:	And her career was in trouble. She came to Louisville to sing at the Kentucky State Fair in 1960, and all of a sudden she was the warm-up act for some teen-ager she'd never heard of named Fabian.
VIVIAN:	Oh, that must have been a bad day. And wasn't she good friends with Robert Kennedy? And she was with him when he got killed?
ASHLEY:	That's awful.
BOBBIE:	Yeah, that's when she really lost it.
ASHLEY:	But she got okay?
BOBBIE:	Better than okay. She came back. She made a lot of records. Good ones, too. Kind of jazzy, American standards stuff. She got awards. And this time around, she picked the songs and sang them the way she wanted to.
ASHLEY:	All right, Rosemary!
VIVIAN:	You know, if Rosemary Clooney could go through all that, and come back and tour around the country in a big shiny dress, singing her heart out and making good money—
BOBBIE:	Maybe there's hope for us yet, is that what you were thinking?
VIVIAN:	Yeah, I mean, she had a lot of problems, the same ones we've had and some more besides.
BOBBIE:	So there is hope.

NELL:	There's always hope, girls.
ASHLEY:	So we should think like Rosemary? There's always better times coming, down the river, around the bend somewhere?
NELL:	You've got to think that, honey.
VIVIAN:	Even if it's not true.
BOBBIE:	But it is true. Good times and bad times both, all mixed up together.
ASHLEY:	Looks like Rosemary Clooney Street runs right down by the river. Can we walk back down there before we go home?
VIVIAN:	I thought we were going to the cemetery.
BOBBIE:	It's whatever you want to do, Mama.
NELL:	I believe I'd rather just go back down to the river a minute. I hate to think about Rosemary in the graveyard, and my own birthday on the tombstone.
VIVIAN:	Rosemary's not in the graveyard, Mama. She's in heaven.
BOBBIE:	Or maybe in purgatory. She said if you really lived your life you'd probably have to spend quite a bit of time in purgatory first.
ASHLEY:	And sounds like she did really live her life.
VIVIAN:	This is why I am glad I'm a Baptist. Something happens, you go straight up to heaven, no waiting around.

Scene 5. The River Again

ASHLEY:	What happened to her?
NELL:	She died. June 29, 2002. She had lung cancer.
VIVIAN:	She smoked a lot.
BOBBIE:	I remember, it was a Saturday night, and I had gone to sleep with the radio on, listening to classical music. When I woke up the next morning there was Rosie singing "Come On-a My House" and I thought, "What a good way to wake up." Then they faded it out and the announcer came on and said, "Rosemary Clooney was 74." And I knew. I got the saddest emptiest feeling. I never even got to see her in person, but I've been watching her my whole life, trying to figure out what there might really be on down the river and where the rocks and the deep waters might be.
ASHLEY:	Did she ever come back here to live?
VIVIAN:	She and Dante bought a house in Augusta, up the river here, where her brother Nick and Nina live.
ASHLEY:	Did she sit on the porch and look at the river?
BOBBIE:	I bet she did.
VIVIAN:	Well, girls, are you all ready to head back to Corbin? We've still got our own lives to live, such as they are.
NELL:	I miss Rosemary. I've always depended on her some way.

BOBBIE: We can still remember her, Mama.

ASHLEY: "Rosemary's for remembrance." That's in Shakespeare. We studied it in English.

VIVIAN: And we can still hear her voice.

BOBBIE: *[Singing.]* In time, the Rockies may crumble, Gibraltar may tumble—they're only made of clay...

ALL: *[Joining in.]* ...But our love is here to stay.

[End.]

AUTHOR NOTE *from playwright* ANNE SHELBY

◇◇◇

I think it was the fall of 2002 when Kathi E.B. Ellis, with
the Pleiades Theatre Company in Louisville, asked me if I'd like to
work with her and others at Pleiades on a new project.

The company had just received an NEA grant
to develop an original collaborative play about Kentucky women.
Louisville playwright Nancy Gall-Clayton and I would develop pieces
separately, Kathi would put them together and direct,
and Sue Massek would write and perform the music.
I thought this sounded like a terrific idea,
and I knew the two Kentucky women I wanted to write about:
Aunt Molly Jackson, the folk singer and union activist,
and singer Rosemary Clooney, who had died only months before.

The results of the collaboration, *Alice Moments: Echoes, Ripples and Light*,
premiered at the Kentucky Center for the Arts in March 2003,
Pleiades' production for Women's History Month.

Later, with support from the Kentucky Foundation for Women,
I developed the short piece I had contributed on Aunt Molly
into a one-woman show, *The Lone Pilgrim*.

I am happy to have out at last the other piece I wrote for *Alice Moments*.
I tried, in this piece, not just to remember Rosemary Clooney
but to suggest some of the ways she had been important to me
and to other women in Kentucky.

Sacred Secrets

bell hooks

Characters:
SISTER RAY   An elderly woman
MAMA ROSA   40s or 50s
GLORA JEAN   20s, MAMA ROSA's daughter

Time: The present
Place: Anywhere
Setting: Two rooms of their house

[At rise, on a dark stage sit three people. In a rocking chair sits the mother, MAMA ROSA. Next to her, her daughter, GLORA JEAN, sits on the stool of a nursing rocker. She holds MAMA ROSA's hand. At a distance from them, as though she is in another room, kneels an elderly woman, SISTER RAY. Light shines on an altar. There are candles, flowers, a big black Bible. We see SISTER RAY as she begins to pray.]

SISTER RAY: O give thanks. O give thanks for the good, for the mercy that endures forever. *[She repeats this line over and over as though chanting it. Light fades leaving SISTER RAY in darkness. Lights come up on MAMA ROSA and GLORA JEAN.]*

MAMA ROSA: My memory ain't what it used to be, you know. Oh, it used to be that I could tell you everything that took place, everything by heart, and you would have felt it just as if you were there.

GLORA JEAN: I wanna hear about Daddy's mama, Sister Ray. Remember, Mama, she came to live with us?

MAMA ROSA: Sick, she was. Too sick to lift a spoon to her lips. And even though she has always done me bad, I took care of her just like she was my own.

GLORA JEAN: That's what I remember most, Mama, that you was so good to her, easing her sickness and easing her dying. I tell everybody Sister Ray was lying there breathing her last in the other room. And all us children knew something way strange was happening 'cause you made us all lie down and take naps. But I was never good at sleeping. I was watching, Mama. And I knew Sister Ray was just gone to glory when you stood there crying quiet like and closed her eyes. Mama, yo' touch was so tender. It was like I could feel it then and I feel it now.

MAMA ROSA: You shouldn't a-been feeling a thing, 'cause your fast butt should have been sound asleep like everybody else. But no, like always, you gotta be watching so you can know and you can tell.

GLORA JEAN: Wasn't much to tell—your closing the eyes. I wanted to know if everybody died with their eyes open, but I knew if I let you know I was watching, I was bound to get punished. Remember, Mama?

MAMA ROSA: No, girl. Like so much else, it's sleeping away.

GLORA JEAN: I can tell you, Mama. It was my first time seeing death, and I see it just like it was yesterday. The middle room — how come we always have a middle room for the sick and dying?

MAMA ROSA: Now, child, that ain't no big secret. The middle room was always closest to where Vee and I was sleeping. So I could hear anybody when they cried out in need. Yes, indeed, so I can hear and come.

GLORA JEAN: That always puzzled me. But I wanna get back on track. I wanna talk more about Sister Ray. That day she died in the middle room, all dark, every curtain closed, you found out I was faking being asleep, because one of the men who came with the stretcher looked right at me, called my name, and laughed saying, "I'm gonna tell on you." And I, not thinking, not even pretending to sleep, pulled the covers up and talked smart, telling him, "Ain't nothing to tell 'cause I did not see."

MAMA ROSA: And there you were, watching, seeing it all. I just did not know what to do, all them whippings must not have changed your mind 'cause here you are, all the way home from college, still trying to know. I ain't never seen no child that wanna know as much. You just don't understand how you worried me something crazy, always fearing that your needing to know would get you hurt—not just beat but maybe kilt. And here you are, just like always, wanting to know, even when my memory just ain't what it used to be.

GLORA JEAN: I just wanna know more about Sister Ray, about Daddy's family. You know they say she had the power, the sight.

MAMA ROSA: Don't I know that better than you? Didn't I live in fear of her seeing, seeing and telling just like you?

GLORA JEAN: *[Laughs.]* I wish I did have the second sight, Mama, 'cause then I really would know everything and not have to ask so many questions.

MAMA ROSA: All while your daddy was courting me, I did not hear a word about her having the sight. Somebody might tell me, "Girl, you better be careful 'cause you don't know what you messing with." But I was young and too good looking for my own good. And your daddy, he was much of a man. What young gal gone turn away from that? Not me. I wanted him to marry me and give me a home, get me away from Baba's house. And he did, even though Sister Ray let me know that she had looked and had seen and we was never gonna have no happiness together.

GLORA JEAN: Was she wrong, Mama? I remember happiness. You and Daddy getting all dressed up to go out. I just would sit and watch. Daddy in a good mood and you looking like a princess. At least then you seemed happy.

MAMA ROSA: Some happiness just not meant. It's like a fly-away feather. No, it's more like the wind you just can't hold onto. It's gonna leave you. Lord, when you feelin' it, you think it's gonna last, but then there comes a day when the feelin' stops and you see. And so it came to me, one day, that his mama had seen it all right. And her seeing had somehow made it all come to pass. I learned bitterness then. I learned hurt.

GLORA JEAN: Oh, but Mama, you did not let it turn you. You were so kind to her. Why, Mama? Why so tender, so careful tending?

MAMA ROSA: 'Cause I got to be a woman. I come into being a grown woman the hard way—'cause I was just a girl when he took me from Baba's house, just a girl with nobody watching and nobody looking out, just a little schoolgirl. I learned that I had been betrayed from the very start, by yo' daddy, by everybody that knew. What they knew was that he was always foolin' with somebody else, some old woman body had already taken his heart. The parts that came to me, the parts that were mine was everything and no good. Yes, baby girl, that happiness was just like the wind. I lived my life in the storms.

GLORA JEAN: You never told him. You never let him see your pain. We never saw your pain.

MAMA ROSA: Oh, but Sister Ray saw it. She saw the pain way before I began to see it and feel it everywhere. Yes, indeed, she saw and she knew—but she also knew I was moving too fast to listen to somebody that done give nothing your way but hate, why I could not hear anything she say with an open mind and heart. That's why I only think it best to stay away from those who say they have second sight. That's why it's hard to answer you when you want to know, baby girl. Sometime knowing bring trouble.

GLORA JEAN: But, Mama, what you telling me, not knowing bring trouble, too. I think it best to know, to see, to see clearly. That's why I believe second sight can make life better, because it helps us see clearly. And I know Sister Ray could see in a sharper, keener way. I want to know whether I can see that way, too. I want to see clearly. *[Lights fade to darkness, then up on SISTER RAY, kneeling at her altar, praying.]*

SISTER RAY: O divine beloved, giver of all good and perfect gifts. This sight I was given I did not want to receive—only make life harder, only give pain. To see too much, to know, give the good blessing but bring, also, the deep hurt. Take from me, beloved, that seeing that causes pain to those who are blind and those who cannot see because they refuse the understanding. Take it from me, all merciful, all powerful one. Let me see only the good, be only a bringer of light. Let this darkness fall off me. It's too heavy for my soul to bear. I talk with spirits and when the spirits say speak, I give vision words. But the world no longer wants to hear. Let me close my eyes now. Let me enter an eternal darkness, a sleep where nothing I see can bring pain.

[End.]

INFORMATIONAL NOTE *about playwright* BELL HOOKS

Born in Kentucky, bell hooks has spent her adult life writing and teaching at such institutions as the University of California at Santa Cruz, San Francisco State University, Yale University, Oberlin College, City University of New York and Berea College in Kentucky. She has written more than thirty books, most dealing with issues related to racial and gender reconciliation.

One Short Sleepe

Naomi Wallace

Character:
BASHEER   Early 20s, Lebanese man

Time: Present
Place: Lebanon
Setting: Outside, digging a grave

[A young Lebanese man, BASHEER, dressed casually, is digging a hole in the ground with a shovel. He digs at different times during the scene but often breaks for periods while speaking to the public.]

BASHEER: At the end of her body. Yes. At the end of her. Body. There are six spinning fingers, called 'spinnerets,' which make a spinning machine so intricate nothing can match it. These fingers, or spinning tubes, having tiny holes at the end of each one through which spills the thread. Spills. I like that word. And I say spills as the spider's web is actually liquid until it comes into. Contact. Into contact with the air. On the feet are tiny claws to guide the thread, three different kinds. And the pilots. Let me tell you about the pilots: when they are very young they climb to the highest points they can find and then turn to face the wind. And there are various kinds of wind. Today, for instance, is the kind of wind the shapes of jets leave behind. When the jets disappear, their silver hangs in the air, their cold fuel floats like blue threads over the city. Nothing

to do with beauty, everything to do with precision. For the spider then
stands on tip-toe, raises its opisthosoma, its abdomen or end, as high as
it can in the air and sends out a stream of silk from its youthful spinnerets. The air takes up the thread and the spinner pays out its line until
it is long enough to tug the spider, and hold its weight. Then the spider
lets go—and pilots the craft through the breeze. And the spider is not
at the mercy of the wind but can haul in its thread or lengthen it to rise
and fall in the air. *[He lets out a celebratory call.]*
This tiny, perfect aircraft may travel long distances, even out to sea, perhaps to
end up on foreign soil. Or if unlucky, to spin its thread on a wave. A
wave.
That's how they came for us.
Wave after wave, the pilots, covering the ground. Covering the ground with
four. Covering the ground with four million. Covering the ground with
four million cluster munitions. Covering our streets, our roofs. The
bombletts lay their hard fruit in the broken road. And they were made
not by God, as the spiders are, but by hands: soldering, cutting, screw-
ing, polishing, testing. And I studied. I studied. Up until the moment
of spinnerets, the spiders and their wonders. Of all the studies I could
have chosen at Beirut University, I chose entomology because spiders
have eight eyes, arranged in two rows on the front of their heads. Eight
eyes, imagine it. Eight opportunities to witness an event at a different
angle.
It was summer. In the year 2006. The jets took off just outside Tel Aviv and
Haifa, perhaps even Jerusalem. And my enemy, my brother the pilot,
pulled the night smooth and tight across our garden while my sister
Ghada examined an ant on her finger. She held the creature up to my
face. 'Get lost!' I said. *[He holds up the blade of the shovel and talks to it
as though it were his sister.]*
"Get lost, Ghada! I'm reading. I have exams tomorrow little girl! You know
nothing about spiders and soon I will know everything!' We were cruel
to each other, my eight-year-old sister and I, because we loved each
other absolutely. I was turning the page of my book on spiders. The
sirens were sounding. The leaflets were dropping. The kindness of
warnings: "You are ordered to evacuate your villages immediately."
We had no weapons in our home. But, ah, the wonder—the wonder of
those tiny spinning tubes, of the liquid, of contact with the air.
It was the second raid. My mother couldn't get back home. She was with her
mother, safe, across town. My dear father was on our roof. His legs
were at the bottom of the stairs. And Ghada had an ant at the end of
her body. At the end of her body, on the end of her finger. And she was
singing or weeping, singing or weeping and I told her to stop but she
just kept on: *[He sings, first in Arabic, then in English.]*

Little Ant, little Ant
God lives in you.
Take me to your home,
The sky's no longer blue.

I said *[He speaks to the shovel-blade again.]*—'Shut up. Sing about spiders, you stupid girl! Not ants. Not ants. Ants can't be pilots.'

The noise of jets is silence. Until they are done. And when they are done, grace closes its door. *[He has finished digging.]*

I was going to be an expert on insects. I read all the books in English. I knew the Latin names for silence, for silly girls, for the numbers that surround the number eight.

The bomb that was falling towards our house, the bomb that was fabricated in Nevada or Wisconsin or Indiana, was dreamt into being through a good day's labor and a good day's work.

And then we were hit.

I wish I had been born a spider. *Chelicera. Epigastric furrow. Spigots.* Such eloquent names for small pieces of the body. And to have eight eyes. Eight eyes to see the world from different vantage points in that half second before death when the sky is clear as cold weather, when the sun is tiny in our throats and we kneel at our graves but cannot not warm the dirt, cannot gather our pieces again, nor explain the absence of the love of strangers whom we have never met, only what they have touched.

My sister Ghada and I. We couldn't hold it together. No. We could not hold it together. Our bodies went in different directions. We were. Dispersed. Yes. We 'kicked the bucket,' we 'bit the dirt,' we 'battened down the hatches.' No. That last one is wrong. Maybe... 'Croaked'? *[He now puts down the shovel and speaks sharply to the grave.]*

'Oh, it wasn't like that, was it? Hey, I've been to University, sister. I know a thing or two. You've got no sense of humor, kid.'

Then you tell me, what were we like when we died? *[He listens to her answer some moments.]*

You are a brat! *[He listens to the grave.]*

All right! All right! *[Beat.]* Ghada says she has eight eyes. Even though she didn't go to University. Even though she never studied spiders! And she says she saw eight things:
One: that we were, both of us, standing side by side, two clear armfuls of water.
Two: that when the bomb dropped down into us, our water leapt from its hold.
Three: that the wind caught us as our liquid made contact with the air.
Four: that we payed out our lines.
Five: we payed out our lines of gossamer thread with the time we had left to us.
Six: that there was a tug at our lines.

Seven: so we let ourselves go. *[He hesitates.]*
What is the eighth thing you saw, Ghada? *[He listens.]*
Huh. She says she won't tell me because I raised my voice. *[He sits on the edge of the gravel hole and examines his work.]*
I have made a good hole. Though not, perhaps, just for us. Not just for myself and Ghada. *[He listens to his sister again.]*
All right. You can have one of my special ink pens if you tell me. But just one. *[He listens again.]*
With the eighth eye my sister says she did not see anything. With the eighth eye in that moment she heard a song. *[To Sister.]* How can you hear with an eye, silly? *[He listens.]* Oh. That's how. Though I am forbidden to tell you. Yet. *[He winks at the audience.]* But I can tell you what she says she heard. *[He listens. Then he sings.]*: Spider, spider, little boy. *[To grave.]* Oh. Sorry. My ears are no longer so good from the blast. *[He speaks to us.]* It's not 'boy.' I try again:
[Sings first in English, then in Arabic.]
Spider, spider, little joy
Who lives in your eyes?
It was so long ago.
It was just yesterday.
Eight times I saw love.
Eight times love saw me.

[End.]

AUTHOR NOTE *from playwright* NAOMI WALLACE

⟡⟡

I created *One Short Sleepe* in response to two things:
Reading John Donne's "Sonnet X," in which I found my title—
"One short sleepe past, we wake eternally, / And death shall be no more;
death, thou shalt die"—and reading Franklin Lamb's brilliant exposé:
*The Price We Pay: A Quarter-century of Israel's Use of American Weapons
Against Civilians in Lebanon, 1978-2006.*

No Time

SALLIE BINGHAM

Characters:
MARYBETH   Middle-aged, a retired school teacher
LOUISE   Middle-aged, a retired school teacher
PAT   Middle-aged, a retired school teacher
X   A young black man

Time: Present
Place: A relatively empty section of a city
Setting: A one-car accident

[At rise, the stage is dark. Sounds of a car engine. Suddenly, a loud crash—then silence. After a beat, lights up. PAT and LOUISE are seated in two chairs, with MARYBETH seated in a chair behind them.]

MARYBETH: Pat? Louise? My God—you all right?
LOUISE: What happened?
PAT: That tire started to make a funny sound, back there—you all hear it? Flip, flop, flip, flop...flip. It was the last flip did it!
LOUISE: Did we have a—
PAT: Blowout! That's what it was—
MARYBETH: You ran us straight into that barricade! Few more feet, we'd be in the river!
PAT: I had my hands LOCKED on the steering wheel!

LOUISE:	I have a great big place here on my knee from ramming into the dashboard.
PAT:	I JAMMED my foot on the brake—we just went into slow motion!
LOUISE:	My horoscope, this morning—it said beware of journeys.
MARYBETH:	I never should have stepped into a car driven by Pat—after all these years—
PAT:	Now don't start blaming me! Anybody can have a blowout.
LOUISE:	*[Rubbing her knee.]* I just couldn't bear to miss one of our Thursday lunches. Haven't missed one in five years.
MARYBETH:	Well, I wish to God I'd missed this one—stayed home and eaten peanut butter out of the jar!
PAT:	But Marybeth, you love our tunafish sandwiches.
MARYBETH:	I never have told you this, Pat—but I hate tunafish!
LOUISE:	My Lord, you two—stop fussing! Nobody's hurt—that's all that matters.
MARYBETH:	I'll get out, flag somebody down—
PAT:	Here in this terrible empty place, under the expressway? Let me see can I get it to start. *[She starts the motor.]*
LOUISE:	Nobody uses this old road anymore to get into town.
PAT:	I just wanted to see the river. *[She backs the car. ALL lurch.]*
LOUISE:	What a horrible noise!
MARYBETH:	Stop that, Pat—you can't drive on a blowout!
PAT:	*[Turning off engine.]* Well, I guess you're right. What are we going to do now?
MARYBETH:	Somebody's bound to come along, sooner or later.
PAT:	No, Marybeth, somebody is NOT bound to come along, and if they do, they'll be the wrong somebody! The right somebodies are all out in the suburbs, where we belong!
LOUISE:	Pat, it was you wanted to come in town for lunch.
PAT:	Yes. I'm sick of all that green!
MARYBETH:	Well, I tell you one thing, I have no intention of sitting here all afternoon. *[She tries to open her door.]* Unlock my door, Pat.
PAT:	No.
MARYBETH:	What do you mean, no?
PAT:	Just no. I pushed my master button the minute we picked you up, Marybeth. I'm responsible for both of you!
MARYBETH:	This is incredible.
PAT:	It's my car. Well, it's Dee's car, but that's the same thing—and I'm responsible for both of you. So nobody gets out of this car 'til I raise my master button. We might as well relax and enjoy ourselves 'til the right somebody comes along.
MARYBETH:	How long do you figure we are going to have to wait?
PAT:	Oh, there'll be a police car here in no time.

MARYBETH:	No time?
PAT:	No time.
MARYBETH:	You ever wonder about that expression?
PAT:	I don't wonder about expressions, generally.
MARYBETH:	Living with Dee Munson has dulled your mind.
LOUISE:	Now, Marybeth!
MARYBETH:	I always did think it meant NO time. I mean, some kind of time that was NO instead of YES.
LOUISE:	This is certainly a fine example of no time. Three old ladies, stranded under the expressway beside the Ohio River!
MARYBETH:	I don't call myself old.
LOUISE:	I do.
MARYBETH:	Do you, Pat?
PAT:	Well, sometimes. When I'm forced to.
MARYBETH:	I don't call myself old.
PAT:	Marybeth, you're only seven years younger than we are—
MARYBETH:	And treasuring every minute of it!
LOUISE:	I don't have a thing in the world against being old—as long as I've provided for my future.
PAT:	I try not to think about my future! Lord, look at those gravel piles—I've never noticed them before.
MARYBETH:	I believe they are sand.
LOUISE:	Yes. Sand.
PAT:	And those mountains of rusty scrap metal—why do they allow that?
LOUISE:	I believe they're mashed cars.
PAT:	Why do they mash them?
MARYBETH:	It's a recognized way of getting rid of the body. You put it in the trunk of the car and then you mash the car.
PAT:	No!
LOUISE:	Now, you two, let's try to think about something else. Charlotte Russe! If help comes in time, we can still go to Plehns Bakery and buy our Charlotte Russe for dessert.
PAT:	They don't close 'til five. That big clock across the river says it's only twelve-fifteen. Dee is looking for me to bring this car home in time for him to start out for the races.
MARYBETH:	Why in the world you won't let me get out and—
PAT:	Dee wouldn't want me to risk a life so he could get to the races!
MARYBETH:	Dee has you under his thumb, Pat—always did! I could understand it if he was good-looking, but Dee Munson is homely as a mud fence.
LOUISE:	Marybeth—show some respect!
PAT:	I should hope I looked deeper than looks, Marybeth, when I looked to marry!

MARYBETH:	You were just as silly—! First boy that asked you, that was it, for life!
PAT:	I resent that! I was an unusually mature twenty-four-year-old when Dee Munson brought me that bunch of white gladiolas!
MARYBETH:	And that was all he ever needed to do.
LOUISE:	Nobody ever brought me white gladiolas.
MARYBETH:	Oh, once they get what they want—
LOUISE:	I've always held onto my respect for the IDEA of marriage, even when—
PAT:	Look, you two! There's the E.T. Slider, going by down the river.
MARYBETH:	Look the other way, you'll see shops.
PAT:	What kind of shops in this no-man's land?
MARYBETH:	Peepshow parlors.
LOUISE:	I thought they knocked all that down with urban removal.
MARYBETH:	That one up on the corner there is a topless shoeshine. *[ALL crane to see.]*
LOUISE:	You spend a lot of time down here?
MARYBETH:	More than the two of you! I believe you've forgotten I'm a big-city girl.
LOUISE:	Just Cincinnati.
MARYBETH:	Well, that counts—!
PAT:	What is a topless shoeshine?
MARYBETH:	I don't know, Pat, but the picture out front shows a naked lady down on her knees over a pair of man's black lace-ups.
LOUISE:	Good Lord.
PAT:	I still don't know what it means.
LOUISE :	Let it go, Pat.
MARYBETH:	Pat was born with a sack over her head.
LOUISE:	Now, Marybeth, that's not kind.
MARYBETH:	I never claimed to be kind. Just pretty!
PAT:	And you sure dress to show it!
MARYBETH:	What are you criticizing now?
PAT:	Those four-inch heels. Thought you'd break your neck, wobbling out to the car.
LOUISE:	Hush, you two! It's worse than the old days at school.
MARYBETH:	Frozen up in the teachers' lounge, or spitting fire. I did most of the spitting.
PAT:	You were mean—!
MARYBETH:	Maybe the biology teacher sees things the English teacher misses. You and your Shelly and Byron.
PAT:	And you and your hideous frogs cut open and splayed out. I admit, I don't like to see anything ugly!
MARYBETH:	That's most of the world.
LOUISE:	I used to love my maps. Pale pink and green and the brightest

shade of yellow—that was the desert. And then of course there were the beautiful oceans. Now they don't teach geography, I wonder what's happened to all those beautiful maps?

MARYBETH: I don't enjoy thinking about frogs, and so forth. The trouble is, though, I try to fix up my thoughts, but it just doesn't do any good.

LOUISE: You're too much by yourself, Marybeth. I get that way when I don't do my volunteer work at the hospital. By the time night comes, I'll be sitting by my window, looking out, and I'll start to think about the days when five o'clock meant a quick change for dinner, fresh lipstick—

PAT: Don't start all that, it's morbid.

MARYBETH: We did have a good time, the three of us, in that stupid old apartment building across from the school.

LOUISE: Took turns making dinner for each other. Sometimes even candles, and flowers. Until you two moved out.

MARYBETH: It just got to be too dreary, Louise, after we retired.

LOUISE: You didn't need to retire, you are seven years younger.

MARYBETH: I didn't want to go on at the school, after you two were gone.

PAT: Dee put up with the three of us long enough—living cheek-by-jowl!

LOUISE: I thought he liked it. He used to love my chicken.

PAT: He liked your cooking better than mine—but he couldn't wait to get us into the house in Saint Matthews. Wanted a yard.

LOUISE: So excited—he wanted everything new!

PAT: Even hired me a cleaning woman. Daisy—came in once a week, did everything, even cleaned the toilet. But I stopped that. I told Dee I wanted to clean my house my own way. Besides—she had a kind of...smell.

LOUISE: Now, Pat, you know that's not true.

PAT: But she did, I tell you

MARYBETH: They offer a cleaning service at my complex. I never have seen the person's face. She comes while I'm at work.

PAT: You can bet she's colored.

LOUISE: You mean black.

PAT: Whatever. It doesn't matter.

MARYBETH: Why is she bound to be...black?

PAT: They all are, that kind of work.

LOUISE: Maybe, but why do you have to say it?

PAT: Does it bother you?

LOUISE: Yes.

MARYBETH: How come?

LOUISE: I was raised by a black woman.

PAT: Well then, Louise, it shouldn't bother you to think about a

	colored woman cleaning toilets. You can be sure yours did that for you.
LOUISE:	It's the way we talk about it. Smells, that kind of thing. But I think...I loved her.
PAT:	Well, I didn't love mine.
LOUISE:	Sometimes I think we love them best of all.
MARYBETH:	That's silly. They're just—
LOUISE:	Hewers of wood and haulers of water.
PAT:	Living high on the hog off the taxpayer—that's what Dee says.
LOUISE:	And freezing to death, somewhere, every cold winter.
MARYBETH:	My heat's included in my rent. Everything's included! Even the use of the tennis courts, and the swimming pool.
LOUISE:	The woman that raised me—I didn't even go to her funeral.
PAT:	Why, nobody would expect you to.
LOUISE:	I expected to.
MARYBETH:	Look—there's somebody over there across the street!
PAT:	Where?
MARYBETH:	[Waving.] Over there! Hey, mister!
PAT:	[Starting to roll down her window, then changing her mind.] I don't believe I'll call. He doesn't look right.
MARYBETH:	Hey, mister! Mister! Roll down my window, Pat!
LOUISE:	Patience, Marybeth.
MARYBETH:	He's gone—didn't even hear me! Why didn't you roll down my window, Pat?
PAT:	I didn't like his looks.
MARYBETH:	You couldn't hardly see him!
LOUISE:	He's gone, anyway.
PAT:	Looked like a little old boy. Our son would be about that age now, if he'd lived.
MARYBETH:	How do you know it was a boy?
PAT:	Dee always wanted a son. He'd be in college now—I'd have insisted on that. Dee didn't go to college. He says it doesn't make a bit of difference. But I'd have wanted our son to know the poets.
MARYBETH:	Even now, after all this time—
PAT:	Why, yes. We still talk about him—gives us something to do instead of looking at television. I mean, something of real interest. We still argue about where we would have sent him to school. Dee was always for the public schools, before busing—then he changed his mind. Started to appreciate OUR little school! We even used to talk about starting a private school for boys, with riflery, things like that.
LOUISE:	You two should have tried again.
PAT:	Oh, I don't know. Seems to me we've enjoyed our son more,

	this way. We never had to deal with that awful rebellion. Dee would have liked to take him to the races, though.
MARYBETH:	He still goes about every day?
PAT:	I tried to stop him, once, but we're closed up together twenty-four hours a day, now that we're both retired. The poor man has to get some fresh air! And you know, when I hear this car start, heading out to the track, I want to shout, "Yes, flee, fly! Fly! Take off and skim over the tops of the trees. And stay away a good long time and spend a lot of money"—because when he does, he's in a good mood at dinner.
MARYBETH:	So that's why you're so hard up.
PAT:	I never said that! What're you doing, Marybeth?
MARYBETH:	Bobbypinning this lock.
PAT:	That'll never work. This car was made right.
LOUISE:	Pat, Honey—you sounded sort of lonely, talking about Dee going to the track.
PAT:	Oh, I'm never lonely. You know, it's kind of funny, but when we slid into that barricade, I thought it was the end.
MARYBETH:	*[Still working on the door lock.]* Nearly was. You nearly hurled us right into the Ohio River.
PAT:	And I just relaxed—went limp as a baby! I thought, Well, now it's over, and we're together, just the way we ought to be, after all these years! Dying seemed like getting finished with another of our lunches. Oh, sorry to say goodbye, maybe, even a little teary, after my one glass of sherry. But not really...sad.
MARYBETH:	Don't you want to end it with Dee?
PAT:	Well, of course I do. But just for a minute there, it seemed like we were closer.
LOUISE:	I know what you mean.
MARYBETH:	*[As bobbypin breaks.]* Damn! What do they make bobbypins out of these days? Used to be you could jimmy any lock—
LOUISE:	You're just going to have to wait, like Pat and me. I expect this is the first time you've had to wait for anything.
MARYBETH :	Now I have to pee.
PAT:	Don't try that on me. I heard you flushing, when I picked you up.
LOUISE:	Even I can last twenty minutes.
MARYBETH:	Dee won't like it if I go on his upholstery.
PAT:	Old age, I'll tell him! People make jokes about it. But I don't really think it's funny—not when I think where it ends. Did you all see, last week in the newspaper, Miss Cameron, the Latin teacher, she fell in Florida and broke her hip? Died.
LOUISE:	You read the obits first thing?
MARYBETH :	Why, what page are they on?

PAT:	I just look to refresh my memory. I have trouble keeping up with names. If I can cross off a few, it makes it easier to remember the rest.
MARYBETH:	You really shouldn't dwell on death. It's unhealthful.
LOUISE:	I was pretty surprised, too, when I started turning to the obits. I thought it was too soon! So I did something about it. I called myself a taxi—
PAT:	Taxi! Why didn't you call me?
LOUISE:	Because I had to go down to Fifteenth and Broadway. That big old woodworking shop where they repaired Mother's highboy. I asked this nice young man to make me a solid mahogany chest, six feet long and three feet wide. Nice young man—such curls! He knew what I wanted.
MARYBETH:	Why, Louise!
LOUISE:	Hear me out. That nice young man looked at me and never said a word. I guess I expected him to argue with me—
PAT:	Why?
LOUISE:	I even made him a little sketch, just to be sure. A nice big chest with simple brass handles on the sides—I thought he'd balk at the handles, but he didn't say a word—
PAT:	Oh, my Lord!
MARYBETH:	How much did it cost?
LOUISE:	You know I don't like to discuss money.
PAT:	Louise, do you mean to say you've got that...thing in your apartment right now?
LOUISE:	Right in back of the big sofa. Next time you come to see me, you'll drop your handbags on it.
MARYBETH:	I'm not squeamish, but I have to admit—
PAT:	Dee would die!
LOUISE:	I expect he would. But it makes a very handsome piece of furniture.
MARYBETH:	Louise—have you ever tried it?
LOUISE:	Why, yes, I have. And I didn't just try it on like a pair of new slacks, either. I waited till a full-moon night and then I lit Mother's silver candelabra, and then I just sort of...slipped in!
MARYBETH:	How did it...fit?
LOUISE:	Just like a glove! I was tempted to get a blanket and spend the night in there.
MARYBETH:	I don't know how I'd feel with something like that in my living room.
PAT:	Dee would never stand for it. I can't even let him know I read the obits. Dee says death is worse than integration!
MARYBETH:	But we do think about it. We just don't talk about it. Death's a dirty word, like masturbation. Everybody does it, but—

PAT:	Why, Marybeth! Who says everybody does it?
LOUISE:	Just the other day, I read a survey—
PAT:	I never trust surveys. Too many people! Half of them are bound to lie.
LOUISE:	It's only normal, after all.
MARYBETH:	Normal! Well, I guess so. I've lived alone for so long, done so many things for myself, I can't afford to be squeamish. The toilets I've unplugged. Drains I've dug out—you never can get a plumber to come in the middle of the night! Chickens I've cleaned— What's masturbating but just another kind of cleaning? What's death, after all, but just another chore? One you're prepared for, Louise.
LOUISE:	There won't be anybody else to deal with it.
PAT:	She's not planning, she's brooding!
LOUISE:	No, I'm not. I'm far too busy for that. I've been brushing up on routes of mass migration, from primitive times to the present. I've been tracing new red lines all over my old atlas. I may take a big trip, after a while!
MARYBETH:	Italy?
LOUISE:	Maybe even Italy.
MARYBETH:	You said you'd never go back.
LOUISE:	Well, I exaggerated. Just because one girl doesn't recognize you—
MARYBETH:	Your prize student, that year. Little Nary Miles Warner. We ran into her in the Duomo, in Florence. In June, you gave her the Silver Acorn Prize in geography, and in early July, in the Duomo, she didn't recognize you.
LOUISE:	That was more than twenty years ago, Marybeth. I've recovered.
PAT:	I guess she didn't expect to see you.
LOUISE:	Yes.
PAT:	You know, frames of reference, and all. After all, how many of them ever invited us to anything after they graduated? Debutante parties, wedding parties? I can count the invitations on the fingers of one hand.
MARYBETH:	They forgot us as fast as they could. I didn't expect anything else.
LOUISE:	You ever think— We had them for those crucial years, thirteen to eighteen, when a girl's tested like metal in the fire. The thin ones, the debutantes, they'd just melt, and marry. Too much heat. Too many choices! But the plain ones, the iron ones, they'd glow red-hot in the fire but they wouldn't lose their form.
MARYBETH:	You always talk like there's something wrong with marrying.
LOUISE:	I never have said that. I respect the idea. The practice,

	though—sometimes it looks a little disappointing.
MARYBETH:	I don't have any complaints about the practice, as long as it's short!
PAT:	What in the world do you mean?
LOUISE:	Now, Pat, don't egg her on.
MARYBETH:	I had a good time with Clement Howe from the minute I walked up to him on the golf course and said, "You look like a man who knows how to hit a ball!"
PAT:	What did HE say?
LOUISE:	I expect he didn't have to SAY anything.
MARYBETH:	You're right, Louise. And he never would have said the words to ask me to marry him, if I hadn't packed my little valise after three solid days of room service! That did it. He begged me to stay.
LOUISE:	He looked worn-out, that time you brought him to the school banquet.
MARYBETH:	He'd started to drink. That was just before the end. Before I ended him, I mean. I just couldn't tolerate his behavior!
PAT:	You never told us he abused you.
MARYBETH:	I guess you couldn't call it abuse.
PAT:	Why, what did he do to you?
MARYBETH:	Nothing. He was just boring.
PAT:	Boring!
MARYBETH:	Out of bed, he had nothing to say for himself. Not too much in bed, either, but that didn't matter. The silent meals! The silent rides in the car! There's not a whole lot of pleasure to be gained, even from a big house in Cincinnati with charge accounts in every store—and two in New York!—when you're paying for it with eternal silence.
PAT:	So what did you do?
MARYBETH:	I packed my little valise again. Quick and clean!
PAT:	Marybeth—you sound almost hard.
MARYBETH:	The English teacher likes romantic poetry. The biology teacher is used to the mess of life! You know, last night, when I went down to the bar in my complex—
PAT:	You go there by yourself?
MARYBETH:	It's just like family, Pat! We speak, we smile—no long conversations, but plenty of short ones. "How was your day?" that kind of thing. The things a husband might ask, coming in the door at night.
PAT:	Aren't they awfully young?
LOUISE:	I always have liked young people.
PAT:	Swinging singles.
MARYBETH:	We may be singles, but we certainly are not swinging. Most

	nights, I'm in bed by ten o'clock.
PAT:	Now, Marybeth, I find that hard to believe.
LOUISE:	Why should you want to believe it?
MARYBETH:	Sure, when I hear there's somebody new in the bar, I make an effort to meet him—who wouldn't? Sometimes, though, when I'm dressing, and I'm already tired, and I think of all the standing up I'm going to have to do in order to lie down in company for a few hours—
PAT:	You don't mean that!
MARYBETH:	I never have minced words with you and Louise.
LOUISE:	There's nothing wrong with the truth.
PAT:	Aren't you afraid of...diseases?
MARYBETH:	The men I meet are all gentlemen—I wouldn't consider any other kind. Sometimes I even find one in church, sitting by himself in a back pew. I can smell the freshness of him, like the air right after a snow—a new man, passing through town. Alone on a Sunday morning, and glad for a home-cooked meal. I always keep spaghetti and sauce on hand.
LOUISE:	You're kind to them.
MARYBETH:	I try.
PAT:	Aren't you embarrassed? I wouldn't want any man outside of Dee to see the state of my stomach!
MARYBETH:	Some of them have stomachs on them, too. And I jog.
PAT:	Does it help?
MARYBETH:	The jogging? Or—?
PAT:	The other.
MARYBETH:	It takes away the fear for a while.
LOUISE:	But it always comes back.
MARYBETH:	Yes.
PAT:	Marybeth, do they ever give you something—afterwards?
MARYBETH:	You mean money?
PAT:	You always have such beautiful clothes.
MARYBETH:	No. They don't give me money. And I don't give them money, either.
LOUISE:	Marybeth, she didn't mean—
MARYBETH:	I don't give a damn what she meant!
PAT:	I didn't mean anything!
MARYBETH:	You're implying I do it for money!
PAT:	I'm not implying anything!
MARYBETH:	You do it with Dee for your keep!
PAT:	WE hardly do it at all.
MARYBETH:	You two think you've found a better way—cleaner! Louise, you live inside your own head. Pat, you live inside some kind of a display of household products. But I'm out—grubbing

	around in the dirty world.
LOUISE:	The inside of my head is not a very clean place.
MARYBETH:	Tell me, you two...ghosts! Did you ever really smell a man? Bury your nose in a male crotch or armpit?
PAT:	That's disgusting!
LOUISE:	I've never had occasion to turn that opportunity down.
MARYBETH:	That's the smell—the stink!—of the real world. Maybe you think you've got the real-world smell in those bottles on your dressing table, Louise. Pat, maybe you think you've caught it in your aerosol cans! But I can tell you, neither one of you knows what the real world smells like, and you never will, because I do it for you. I bury my nose in...things! For you!
PAT:	But we never asked you to do that! I don't WANT you to do that—
MARYBETH:	You've known it, all along! Every time we get together, you can't wait to hear what dirtiness I've been up to—can't wait to ask me for all the details, so you can cluck and shake your head. I know why you ask! You're starving for it—
LOUISE:	*[Reaching across PAT to push the master button.]* All right, Mary beth. The doors are unlocked.
MARYBETH:	High time! I can't spend any more time with ghosts! *[She gets out of the car.]*
LOUISE:	You're right. Flesh-and-blood can't be friends with ghosts.
PAT:	Close the door! I'm pushing the button again. *[She does so.]* Now she's out there alone on the street. *[MARYBETH crosses the stage.]* Oh, look, Louise—there's somebody over there! *[X, a good-looking young black man, wearing an overcoat, enters and stands watching MARYBETH. She beckons to him.]* And she's beckoning to him! This is dangerous, Louise—let her back in! *[She honks the horn.]* Marybeth! Come on back! *[MARYBETH, talking to X, ignores PAT.]*
LOUISE:	She belongs out, Pat. She's not coming back. Besides, maybe that man can help us.
PAT:	Louise, that's a colored man, you know that, and we don't know anything about him, here in no-man's land—and Marybeth's out there talking to him!
LOUISE:	Nothing we can do about it now.
PAT:	They're coming this way! I don't like that overcoat, Louise. Why is he wearing an overcoat?
LOUISE:	It's cold out.
PAT:	THEY don't care! THEY don't even feel the cold, when their blood is up!
X:	*[Inspecting the car.]* Looks like you got a blow-out. That tire is gone.

MARYBETH:	Can you do something about it?
X:	I don't know nothing about cars.
MARYBETH :	We'll pay you.
X:	I don't want money. You got a jack and a spare in the trunk?
MARYBETH:	I don't know, it's not my car. My friend's husband is bound to keep all the equipment—
X:	But how you going to get at it? That's always the question! You got all the equipment in the world, but how you going to get at it?
MARYBETH:	*[Knocking on car window.]* Pat! Pass the car keys out. We have to get in the trunk.
PAT:	No! *[As LOUISE reaches for the car keys.]* Don't you dare! This key opens the door, too!
MARYBETH:	Louise! We need the keys!
LOUISE:	Sorry—I can't do anything.
X:	*[To MARYBETH.]* Don't your friends want to be saved?
MARYBETH:	Of course they do! We've been waiting a long time.
X:	I know. I saw you.
MARYBETH:	Saw us? From where?
X:	I was watching.
MARYBETH:	All the time we were waiting?
X:	White women always waiting. You better get me those keys.
MARYBETH:	They're too scared.
X:	You scared, too?
MARYBETH :	No. I'm never scared.
X:	*[Taking her hand.]* Then how come you trembling?
MARYBETH:	I'm cold. I left my coat in the car.
PAT:	Oh Lord, Louise! Look—what's he doing to her?
LOUISE:	He's holding her hand.
PAT:	And she's letting him! I always knew Marybeth—
LOUISE:	Hush.
X:	*[To MARYBETH.]* You always cold.
MARYBETH:	Are you trying to tell me something?
X:	Maybe. I'm a preacher.
MARYBETH:	You are? That's wonderful! What is your church called?
X:	The Church of All Outdoors.
MARYBETH:	I've never heard of that.
X:	We're on the radio.
MARYBETH:	I'll have to listen to you. When are you on?
X:	All the time. You're still trembling.
MARYBETH:	I'm still cold.
X:	You want my coat?
MARYBETH:	No!
X:	You looking at me funny. What's the matter with you?

MARYBETH: That coat. It looks like you don't have anything on, underneath.

X: You want to check me out?

MARYBETH: No! I'll take it on faith—

X: What faith?

MARYBETH :   Who are you?

X: Nobody. I'll open this coat up, if you want.

MARYBETH: No! I believe you!

X: Believe what?

MARYBETH: I believe you've got something on, underneath.

X: Do you believe I'm a preacher?

MARYBETH :   Yes! I believe that!

X: Why?

MARYBETH: Look, my mother always told me—

X: Didn't she tell you to watch out for black men in overcoats?

MARYBETH: That wasn't me, that's my friend, in the car. She was raised by— My mother was all I had, and she was, well, of course, she used to say— Look, my friend, sitting there in the car, she was raised by—

X: I know. And she was more her mother than her mother was. She loved her.

MARYBETH: Yes. I mean, really! She really did!

X: Is she still living? The one that raised your friend?

MARYBETH: I don't believe so. I believe she passed away some years ago.

X: Your friend went to her funeral?

MARYBETH: Well, she meant to, but I believe she was out of town.

X: She didn't go to her funeral?

MARYBETH: What is this? What are we talking about?

X: Salvation.

MARYBETH: What?

X: Getting your car fixed. So she didn't go to her funeral.

MARYBETH: Look, I don't know. I don't remember, really. What difference does it make?

X: *[Pointing to PAT.]* Your other friend, there, what does she do?

MARYBETH: She's retired.

X: Does she scrub out her own toilet?

MARYBETH: Why, I believe she... For a while, she had...

X: Yeah.

MARYBETH: Look, they're both good women. Why do you have to know all this?

X: Got to know who it is I'm helping. What about you? What do you do?

MARYBETH: I don't do anything.

X: Nothing? The whole time?

MARYBETH:	What are you asking me?
X:	You want to be saved, or not? *[He begins to unbutton coat.]*
MARYBETH:	Of course I want to be saved!
PAT:	My Lord! Look at that!
LOUISE:	He'll stop. I know he'll stop.
MARYBETH:	Look, I never claimed to do anything. I just got by, like everybody else. Please—don't unbutton that any further.
X:	Just...got by. But you the one wants to see everything. Wants to touch everything! Smell everything! Ain't that so? *[He unbuttons another button.]*
MARYBETH:	I was just trying to explain to them—
X:	*[Unbuttoning another button.]* Don't you want to see?
MARYBETH:	No!
X:	Don't you want to touch?
MARYBETH:	Not anymore—
X:	Don't you want to...smell?
MARYBETH:	*[Turning her back.]* Please. Just go away. We'll find somebody.
X:	But I can save you.
MARYBETH:	I know you can.
PAT:	Oh Lord, he's stopped! He's still got one more button to go! Can you lip-read, Louise?
LOUISE:	I'm trying, but I can't get anywhere. Pat, do you know how to pray?
PAT:	Of course I know how to pray.
LOUISE:	Then start.
PAT:	Now I lay me down to sleep, I pray the Lord my soul to keep. Four angels guard my bed, two at the foot, two at the—
LOUISE:	Our father who art in heaven—
X:	*[To MARYBETH.]* I can save you. But I got to want to.
MARYBETH:	I said we'd pay.
X:	I don't want money.
PAT:	Louise, he's going to get her to DO something. *[She rolls down the window.]* Marybeth! Don't bargain with the devil! *[She rolls up the window again.]*
LOUISE:	Thy will be done, on earth as it is in heaven—
PAT:	Don't say that, Louise! You'll make it happen!
MARYBETH:	*[To X.]* If you're a preacher, you ought to help us out of charity. Three helpless women.
X:	Three rich white bitches.
MARYBETH:	I'm not rich. I work part-time behind the cosmetics counter, selling lipstick.
X:	The other two are.
MARYBETH:	Pat lives off her pension. Louise—
X:	That's the one!

LOUISE:	Give us this day our daily bread—
MARYBETH:	What does money have to do with it?
X:	*[Pointing at LOUISE.]* Tell her to get out of the car.
MARYBETH:	She won't.
X:	Try.
MARYBETH:	No.
X:	I can't help just one. I got to help all three. You need me. You gotten to the end of the jumping off place, Marybeth.
MARYBETH:	*[Knocking on the window.]* Louise!
LOUISE:	She wants me to get out.
PAT:	I'm not unlocking the door!
LOUISE:	She wants me to help her. Unlock the door, Pat.
PAT:	No.
LOUISE:	If you let me out, you can stay inside. I'll arrange it.
PAT:	You promise?
LOUISE:	Yes. Unlock the door.
PAT:	*[Pushing the master button.]* Get out—quick! *[LOUISE gets out. PAT relocks doors.]* Matthew Mark Luke and John, guard the bed I lie upon.
MARYBETH:	Louise, this is—
LOUISE:	How do you do. Are you going to help us? It's getting late.
X:	Almost the end, Louise.
LOUISE:	*[To MARYBETH.]* Did you tell him my name?
MARYBETH:	He says he was watching.
LOUISE:	*[To X.]* What are you going to do?
X:	You all want to get home before dark, ask that other one, in the car, to get out.
MARYBETH:	She'll never get out.
X:	Tell her.
LOUISE:	She won't listen.
X:	*[Taking hold of MARYBETH.]* Tell her I will let loose of her friend if—
LOUISE:	*[Knocking on window.]* Pat! Get out!
PAT:	*[Covering her eyes.]* God bless America, land that I love.
LOUISE:	Pat!
PAT:	Stand beside her and guide her.
MARYBETH:	No use, Louise.
LOUISE:	*[To X.]* She's praying. She won't listen to me.
X:	*[Letting go of MARYBETH.]* Well, you tried. *[He takes a key out of his pocket, fits it in the car door lock and opens it.]* Step right on out, little lady.
PAT:	*[Uncovering her eyes.]* I can't. I'm too scared.
X:	I'll help you. *[He helps PAT out of the car.]*
PAT:	Why, thank you! You remember the old L&N railroad? Those

	porters always had a little steel step they'd put down, under the door, and then they'd reach up and help you out. When I was a little girl, we used to go to Florida—
X:	Now. Looks like you three ladies need some help.
PAT:	Yes, we do! Are you going to help us?
MARYBETH:	There's a pay phone up the street, if you'll just let us—
LOUISE:	We could call Triple-A.
PAT:	*[To X.]* I wasn't really afraid of you. It was just that coat. The porters on the old L&N always wore these nice clean white jackets.
MARYBETH:	Please let us go up there and use the pay phone.
X:	I'll be glad to take you ladies on up the street. I'll even wait to see if the man do what you want him to do, cause we all know the white man can be ornery. *[ALL laugh.]* But before we start on that long walk, I want to show you ladies something I believe you been waiting to see. Waiting a long time! I'm going to show you because we are all the Children of God.
PAT:	Why, what are you going to show us?
MARYBETH:	I don't want to see anything right now.
LOUISE:	I'm curious.
X:	You all curious, closed up inside your white walls and burning with curiosity! You never had a chance to satisfy it. Never had a chance to put out that fire. I'm going to give you that chance, today. After today, you won't have to burn up with curiosity anymore.
PAT:	Why, what do you mean to do?
LOUISE:	Be quiet, Pat.
MARYBETH:	I'm not curious at all.
X:	Don't be afraid. *[X unbuttons the last button on his overcoat. He holds the coat open. He is wearing a pair of white underpants with red hearts printed on them.]* There, you see? Love. That's all there is to it. *[PAT hides her eyes. LOUISE looks closely. MARYBETH turns to run.]* Marybeth, wait now. *[POLICE SIREN is heard offstage.]*
PAT:	They're coming to help us! *[Shouting.]* Yoohoo! Over here!
LOUISE:	Don't call them, Pat!
MARYBETH:	*[To X.]* Get out of here.
X:	I don't run. *[He drops the coat to the ground.]*
BULLHORN:	*[Offstage.]* HIT THE DECK! HIT THE DECK! ONE, TWO THREE! ONE, TWO THREE! EENY, MEANY, MINY, MO! CATCH A ... HIT THE DECK! ONE POTATO, TWO POTATO! HIT THE DECK! *[MARYBETH, LOUISE and PAT lie on the stage.]*
X:	*[Turns to face the BULLHORN, smiling.]* Just remember, you

are all saved. Children of God...
BULLHORN: *[Offstage.]* BY THE TOE! *[Automatic gun fire. X falls. A pause.]*
MARYBETH: *[Raising her head.]* Pat? Louise? My God—you all right?
[End.]

AUTHOR NOTE *from playwright* SALLIE BINGHAM

I wrote *No Time* to commemorate my high school teachers,
devoted unmarried women who started me on my road as a writer.
I wondered what might have happened to them after they retired,
when the times were changing and affecting
their habits and ideas in startling ways.
Then, I wanted to put them into a time capsule,
a car that would insulate them—almost—
from the changed world around them.
And I wanted to break with the rules of realism
to bring them to a startling conclusion.

Afterword

"The Presence of Us"

Historically, in most of the world, the presence of women in theatre was unthinkable (except when we occupied space as customers). Such an archaic notion seems exceptionally nutty to us these days, but more likely than not, nothing would have changed if not for women themselves insisting on taking our rightful seats at the thespian banquet. There have been breakthroughs and setbacks, but over time things have changed…dramatically.

The 21st century is a time when women not only write scripts, we also produce them, we act in them, we design tech for them, we are dramaturgs and directors, publishers, agents and marketers. And women own theatres, too.

We are a very long way from the days when women weren't allowed to set foot backstage or, heaven forbid, onstage. Now, of course, the whole theatre is ours, from front of house, to the boards and wings, to catwalk and booth and scene shop.

To the credit of the great-great-grandsons of the old guard, men never even think to be resentful about the presence of us in theatre today. Perhaps this is because women have long since proven our value in theatre and everywhere else once denied us. Or perhaps it is because today's men are more intrigued, more emotionally invested than ever before in the successes of their daughters, their partners, their mothers and sisters, their colleagues and collaborators.

The significance of all this change stems from women being both contenders and contributors. *Scenes from the Common Wealth* collects a handful of representative pieces into an important document of theatre work published at a time when women have spent the last three generations deliberately changing the face of theatre (and nearly everything else) around the globe. Women have been, for a long time, shifting gears and gaining traction through a movement in which we sometimes found—but more often created—ways to ensure that our public voices could emerge in powerful ways.

The accomplished Lillian Hellman was notably on the forefront of competing with men who wrote during her era. Nevertheless, and in spite of her many successes, it was primarily those men (Eugene O'Neill, Arthur Miller and Tennessee Williams, for example) who then and for years afterward sprang immediately to mind as indelible American playwrights of the 1930s-60s. Since that time, things have shifted. Now a number of women who write plays are just as likely to endear themselves to fans and followers. Think Kentucky's own Marsha Norman. Think Beth Henley, Paula Vogel, Wendy Wasserstein.

History is filled with men's stories written by men. But the greater truth is this: The entire history of humankind literally pivots on the presence of us.

What much of the rest of the world doesn't know is that our state has been one of the places where this gender shift, in the arts anyway, has been quite active. Even in rural areas of this Commonwealth, women are deeply involved in theatre and other art forms, and this has accelerated in part because we have been endowed with a unique service organization that has designed its mission around making it possible for women to put those two life-altering and culture-changing forces—art and activism—to use for the common good. Art first meets activism in this part of the world at an intersection called the Kentucky Foundation for Women, a grant-making non-profit established here in 1985.

Let it be noted, in fact, that a number of women in this collection have, in one way or another, been directly involved with KFW, and many have been recipients of its generosity. In fact, a few of the pieces in this book were written during workshops or retreats funded by KFW. Once seeds are planted, all manner of blossoms, fruit, nourishment and perpetuation follow. It's an intellectually organic process.

Opportunities such as these not only assist the artistic work a woman wants to do but also change the mindset of the individual artist about what she *can* do. And though the natural ripple effect—however slight or grand—to other parts of the nation and the world are impossible to measure, they do exist, for we all are connected.

The entire world's culture has been markedly evolving. The work of women artists, especially those who long struggled to be heard and rewarded for our contributions, isn't always about the women or even about the art. It is about our progress as a state, as as a nation, as a populated planet. Some of the playwrights in this collection have created international theatre art. This probably wouldn't have happened a few generations ago, at least not at current levels. We must maintain our artistic presence in the world and keep these voiced gains from back-sliding under the pressure of all insidious and outright forms of political madness defining our present time.

We who have worked on *Scenes from the Common Wealth* have been conscious of representing various types of playwrights who have created their work across our state, from west to east…and beyond. We've included scripts by women from the mountains, from the bluegrass and from Kentucky's delta on the state's west coast. Work came to this collection across oceans and deserts, too. We've sought plays from urban and rural women. Perhaps writers in this book have been temporary Kentuckians; perhaps they have stayed for a lifetime. Plays from those who live here now, those who don't, and those who left and then returned represent diverse life experiences, interests and points of view.

We've also been deliberate in including lesser-known or first-time writers alongside well-established playwrights who have ties to our state, sometimes as daughters, sometimes as residents. Some of the best and most enduring qualities of the more seasoned writers in this collection give example to what the emerging writers hope to develop in their own work over time. Those women who have mastered the art of playwriting are willing to stand witness, shoulder-to-shoulder, with the efforts of the newer voices in this book. Whether or not these and other brilliant artists who have achieved acclaim think of the rest of us very often, we think of them. And we call them our sisters, for they are artists and activists and writers of wisdom. They are thinkers and role models who inspire us and whose work we relate to, women we recognize as being, in important ways, part of the presence of us. Where the experienced playwrights meet the novices in this collection, they share this simple wrinkle: A piece of each writer's artistic journey has included Kentucky.

This anthology is a representative slice of history—not just these contributors' histories but your history too. This book does not claim to include everything, but it's a start, it's a reminder of this challenging journey we're on, and it's a way to set one more milepost along the way…so that others can find us and follow, bringing their best as they come.

With projects of this nature, taking the long view is important: This book may very well hold even greater value years hence that it does right now. But for the present day it is enough that *Scenes from the Common Wealth: Short Plays & Monologues by Kentucky Women* serves to document, in part, yet another hard-won shift in our cultural history.

The scope of a wave can be difficult to detect when we're swept along inside it, yet the passing of time will prove true these things: Creative potential is realized in our collective intellectual motion, and mind-opening power dwells in the very presence of us.

KATE LARKEN is, among other identities, a publisher and a playwright. Kate's scripts include *Teddy's Piece* (co-writer), which toured off-and-on for about a dozen years, was voted season's Best Play at Actors Guild (1998), and was later published in a literary edition (MotesBooks, 2011); *Going Up Home* and *Don't Think Twice*, both of which were developed and produced as staged readings in the Kentucky Voices new plays series at Horse Cave; *Beyond Aprons: The Legacy of Portland Women*, a monologue/radio series commissioned by the Portland Museum; several short plays and numerous monologues. She's at work on a script inspired by the voice poems of a Kentucky woman, the late Lee Howard.

About the Playwrights

ARLENE HUTTON is best known for *The Nibroc Trilogy: Last Train to Nibroc* (Drama League Best Play Nomination), *See Rock City* (In the Spirit of America Award) and *Gulf View Drive* (LA Weekly and Ovation Award nominations). Works include *As It Is In Heaven* and *Letters to Sala.* Her plays have been presented Off- and Off-Off Broadway, in London and throughout the world, including four times at the Edinburgh Festival Fringe. She is a six-time ATL ten-minute play finalist and three-time Samuel French Short Play winner. Arlene is an alumna of New Dramatists and a member of Ensemble Studio Theatre and Dramatists' Guild.

BRENDA K. WHITE lives in Somerset, Kentucky. She has an M.A. in social work and in English and is currently employed by the University of Kentucky Center on Drug and Alcohol Research. She has written and published poetry, short stories, essays and articles in various journals and anthologies. Her poem, "Last Suppers, 1998," was published in the *Seattle Journal for Social Justice.* She was also published in *Poetry as Prayer.* Brenda has written a monologue about Cornblossom, the last Cherokee Chief living in south-central Kentucky. She lives with her husband and their seven dogs.

DENISE R. MCKINNEY is spiritual director for Selah Circle, facilitating safe space where one can commune with God and self. She holds a graduate degree in Pastoral Care and Counseling and undergraduate degrees in Psychology and Child Development. Her writing has garnered awards from Kentucky Arts Council and Kentucky Foundation for Women, most notably the grant that enabled her to compile and edit a poetry anthology, *Poetry as Prayer: Appalachian Women Speak* (Wind Publishing, 2004). Residing in Berea, Kentucky, Denise combines her interests in writing, spirituality, healing and dream interpretation to inform her work and play.

BETH DOTSON BROWN is an award-winning short story writer whose work has been published in *Quality Women's Fiction, St. Anthony Messenger, Branchwood Journal* and has aired on the BBC World Service Short Story Programme. Her compilation of three short plays, *Mothers, Daughters, and the Space in Between*, all originated as short stories. She has also written several short plays for youth performances. Beth freelances as a writer and editor, works as an artist-in-residence with students, and consults on communications for non-profits. Her first book, *Yes! I am Catholic*, was published by St. Mary's Press in 2007. Contact her at www.bethdotson-brown.net.

BELINDA MASON In addition to her play, *The Gifts of the Spirit,* Belinda Mason wrote a number of short stories, which are housed in Special Collections at the University of Kentucky. Belinda grew up in Letcher County, graduated from UK with a degree in journalism, and later wrote and lived in western Kentucky (Hartford and Utica) with her husband and two children. She died in 1991.

CONSTANCE ALEXANDER is a poet, playwright, fiction writer, independent producer and newspaper columnist. Author of two poetry chapbooks; a memoir, *Who Needs June Cleaver?*; and two spoken operas, *Kilroy Was Here* and *The Way Home*; she edited two anthologies of writings by union workers, *Kindred Voices I* and *II* (University of Massachusetts). *Last Call* is featured in *Art of the One-Act* (University of Western Michigan). She has received grants and fellowships from Kentucky Foundation for Women, Kentucky Arts Council, Newspaper Association of America, Pew Center for Civic Journalism, Ragdale Foundation, and Poets & Writers Inc. Writers Exchange.

LIZ FENTRESS is an award-winning playwright, director and actor. In Louisville, she acts for Stage One Family Theatre and is a teaching artist for Actors Theatre of Louisville's New Voices program. Previously, Liz worked at Horse Cave Theatre, coordinating the Kentucky Voices program for the development of new plays by or about Kentuckians. She co-edited the anthology *World Premieres from Horse Cave Theatre* (MotesBooks, 2010). Prior to moving to Horse Cave, Liz was director of Playhouse in the Park in Murray, where she founded the West Kentucky Playwrights. Liz's plays have been produced across the U.S. and staged in London's West End. She has received playwriting awards from North American Actors Association, National Educational Television Association, Kentucky Arts Council, and Kentucky Foundation for Women. Visit Liz's website at www.lizfentress.com.

NANCY GALL-CLAYTON was Tennessee Williams Scholar at Sewanee Writers Conference and Visiting Artist at Ohio State University. *General Orders No. 11* won the Streisand Festival of New Jewish Plays, *The Colored Door at the Train Depot* won the Heritage Festival, and *Just Taking Up Space* appeared in *World Premieres from Horse Cave Theatre* (MotesBooks, 2010). More than fifty of her plays have been on stages across the country and in Australia and Canada. Nancy chaired the High School Play Contest for the Southeastern Theatre Conference. She belongs to the Dramatists Guild and the International Centre for Women Playwrights.

GAIL LIVESAY is a writer of poetry, essay, plays, fiction and non-fiction. Many of her pieces deal with bipolar disorder. Her poetry is published in *Poetry as Prayer, Appalachian Women Speak, The Seeker,* and *Appalachian Connection.* She writes regularly for area newspapers, educating readers about bipolar disorder. Her play, *Ward 101*, received its first public reading at Second Fridays, sponsored by Berea Arts Council. Her memoir, *Little Girl Inside*, is also published. Gail was a participant in the first Kentucky Women Playwrights Seminar, funded by Kentucky Foundation for Women.

CAROLYN BERTRAM-ARNOLD has published over 100 pieces, including poetry, short stories and personal essays, several published more than once. Her writing has appeared mainly in regional magazines such as *Appalachian Heritage, Back Home in Kentucky,* and *Appalachian Women's Journal,* but a few poems and essays have gone national/international with *Byline, The Writer's Journal,* and online at usadeepsouth.com. Although fairly new to playwriting, two of her 10-minute plays have been performed in Berea, Kentucky, as part of larger productions. She lives a semi-quiet country life with her best friend/husband Jack in Livingston, Kentucky.

LINDA CALDWELL'S play, *Homespun,* was produced at Berea College's From Page to Stage Festival of New Plays. *Flatboat on the Ohio*, was produced at Artists Collaborative Theatre in Elkhorn City, Kentucky, during the first Kentucky Women Playwrights Festival. A short play, *Katrina and the Lord Have Mercy Clothes Closet*, was a runner-up for Appalachian Writers Association's Josefina Niggli Playwriting Award. *How to Make Like a Crazy Quilt* was produced for Berea Arts Council's Quilt Extravaganza. *Aunt Jerusha* was produced at Berea Arena Theater during a Kentucky Women Playwrights Seminar production of *Nine Characters in Search of an Audience*. Linda writes plays and poetry on a farm near Paint Lick, Kentucky.

TRISH AYERS' plays have had readings/productions throughout the United States and Japan including: *Live Girls!,* Hedgerow Theatre; Iowa State University; Lute Hall, Biwa-Cho, Japan; Berea College; Bard's Town Theatre; Western Illinois University; Berea Arena Theater and Manhattan Theatre Source. Awards include Appalachian Writers Playwriting Awards, playwriting grants, and the 2011 Sallie Bingham Award from the Kentucky Foundation for Women. Trish's plays have been finalists in Heartland Ten-Minute and One-Act Play Festivals and in Roots of the Bluegrass New Play Contest. She is a member of the Dramatists Guild and founder/director of Kentucky Women Playwrights Seminar.

ANNE SHELBY'S plays have been performed at venues such as Appalshop, Pleiades Theatre, University of Kentucky, Eastern Kentucky University, Lincoln Memorial University and Georgetown College's Kentucky Onstage series. They include a one-woman show, *The Lone Pilgrim: Songs and Stories of Aunt Molly Jackson*; a finalist in Barter Theatre's Festival of Appalachian Playwrights, *Passing Through the Garden: The Work of Belinda Mason*; and the project for which *Remembering Rosemary* was written, *Alice Moments: Echoes, Ripples and Light,* in collaboration with Pleiades. A storyteller and resident of southeastern Kentucky, Shelby has also authored poems, children's books and newspaper columns, collected as *Can A Democrat Get Into Heaven? Politics, Religion and Other Things You Ain't Supposed to Talk About* (MotesBooks, 2006).

bell hooks is currently a distinguished professor in residence in Appalachian Studies at Berea College. A world renowned author, cultural critic, poet, feminist theorist and essayist, she has published widely. Most recently, she published the book of essays, *Writing Beyond Race,* and an award winning book of poetry, *Appalachian Elegy*, published by the University Press of Kentucky. She lives in Berea, Kentucky.

NAOMI WALLACE'S work has been produced in the United States, the United Kingdom, the Middle East and Europe. She has received the Susan Smith Blackburn Prize, the Kesserling Prize, the Fellowship of Southern Writers Drama Award, an Obie, and the MacArthur "Genius" Fellowship. Some of her plays include *One Flea Spare, In the Heart of America, The Trestle at Pope Lick Creek, Things of Dry Hours, The Hard Weather Boating Party* and *And I and Silence.* Her award-winning films, co-written with Bruce McLeod, include *Lawn Dogs, The War Boys* and *Flying Blind.* In 2012, Naomi received the Horton-Foote award for most promising new American play for *The Liquid Plain.* She is the inaugural recipient for the 2013 Windham Campbell prize for drama.

SALLIE BINGHAM published her first book, a novel, two years after graduating from Radcliffe College and in the years since then has published seven novels, four collections of short stories, many plays, and a memoir. Her most recent book, *Mending: New and Selected Stories* was published by Sarabande Books in 2011. In 2014, Sarabande Books will publish *The Blue Box: Three Lives in Letters*, a nonfiction narrative based on the lives of Sallie's great-grandmother, her grandmother and her mother, spanning the mid-19th century to the mid-20th century. She has lived in Santa Fe since 1991.

www.ingramcontent.com/pod-product-compliance
Lightning Source LLC
Chambersburg PA
CBHW071229090426
42736CB00014B/3019